LITTLE FLOWER

RECIPES FROM THE CAFE

CHRISTINE MOORE

Published by Prospect Park Books, an imprint of Prospect Park Media
969 S. Raymond Avenue
Pasadena, California 91105
prospectparkmedia.com

Library of Congress Cataloging in Publication Data

Moore, Christine, 1963-
 Little Flower : recipes from the café / by Christine Moore — 1st ed.
     p. cm.
 ISBN 978-0-9834594-8-4
1. Cooking, American. 2. Little Flower (Restaurant) I. Title.
 TX715.M822 2012
 641.5973--dc23

                                        2012015108
 ISBN: 978-0-9834594-8-4

First edition, first printing

Designed by Rachel Vourlas Schacht
Front cover design by Eric Pfleeger

Printed in China

ADVANCE PRAISE

"Like most things worth having, Christine Moore's sea salt caramels sting for a moment before dissolving into pure, buttery happiness. And I can't begin to count the mornings I've slipped into her café for a quick pie crust cookie and ended up chatting until noon about the the thermodynamics of marshmallows. You can't always have Christine Moore around to explain her perfect blood orange tarts, but Little Flower may be close enough."
— *Jonathan Gold, Pulitzer Prize–winning food writer and columnist for the* Los Angeles Times

"Fans of Christine Moore and her café, myself included, can rejoice! She has put together a charming cookbook that needs to be left in the kitchen, not on the bookcase. The recipes are so clearly written and so fun—you just know they're going to turn out good. And I love the back story about Christine and her dream coming true."
— *Nancy Silverton, founder of La Brea Bakery, owner of Mozza, and author of many cookbooks*

"Little Flower's food, like Christine Moore herself, is nuanced yet playful, seasoned and balanced, crafted but honest. It's the food we eat when we're craving nourishment as well as when we want to celebrate. Little Flower Cafe is a gem of a shop, and now Christine has created a gem of a book."
— *Kim Boyce, James Beard–award winning author of* Good to the Grain *and owner/baker of Bakeshop in Portland, Oregon*

"Christine Moore has filled her café with such delicious goodness and friendly warmth that it is the place to go to nourish the body and soul. In this delightful book, Christine shares with us her sweet and savory recipes so that we can whip up some Little Flower charm at home."
— *Jeanne Kelley, author of* Salad for Dinner *and* Blue Eggs and Yellow Tomatoes

"Reading Christine Moore's book drifted me back to the mid-1990s, when she casually wandered into my first wine shop in Paris and struck up a conversation in what she believed was French. We still have a good laugh about it. Now she's turned that same warmth and boundless energy toward creating a wonderful cookbook, using winding back roads instead of the well-traveled freeway. Her spirit and vision led her to create recipes in such a simple and personal manner. This is a refreshing approach to food in a world of overcomplicated chefs."
— *Juan Sanchez, owner/chef of the Paris restaurants Fish and Semilla and the wine shop La Dernière Goutte*

For Madeline, Avery & Colin

maple
oat

H
Lav
so

TABLE OF CONTENTS

Little Flower is my life's dream. A tiny café on the edge of town, it's where we gather to prepare and eat fresh, delicious food, drink strong coffee, listen to great music, and surround ourselves with art, neighbors, friends, and community.

The café was born in 2007. That was a really tough year. My candy business had gone into storage because of an unrenewable lease. I had been dealing with an unexpected and difficult pregnancy. At 44, I found myself with a premature baby, a broken marriage, a 5-year-old, a 7-year-old who had just been diagnosed with Tourette Syndrome, a husband out of work, cancelled health insurance, and no way to pay the mortgage.

My great friend Sumi Chang, who owns Pasadena's Euro Pane bakery and café, called me on a Monday night to tell me about a little bakery that had just closed. I wrote a note about myself and my candy business and drove there in the dark that very night. I slipped my note under the door, where it joined a huge pile of forgotten mail.

The next day, the phone rang. It was Byron and Loree McIntyre, the owners of the building and the closed bakery. We met immediately, and for some reason they took a chance on me. With the incredible support of my parents, Craig Cooper and Barbara Sheridan, I had the keys two days later, and Little Flower was reborn. There was cleaning and painting to be done, and with the help of my friend Oi Lam, we opened in a mere two weeks and were making caramels and marshmallows in time for Christmas.

I spent many days and nights alone in that beautiful kitchen with the long brick wall. I'd always dreamed that my own place would have a brick wall. Sometimes when I'd look at that wall, I'd cry with gratitude. My dreams were coming true. I'd bake all night and go up front to man the counter for coffee and pastry duty. Within a few months, I was making a few sandwiches and feeling my way around this new business. The neighborhood was incredible. I know most regulars don't know how many nights I was on my knees in that kitchen, praying for this to work so I could support my family and keep my house. There were many days when I wasn't sure we'd succeed, but with the support of the dearest of friends, like Pam Perkins, and the most incredible crew in the world, we are celebrating our fifth year. Our menu has expanded to include soups, salads, bowls, quiches, tarts, breakfast dishes, and many baked goods. And now we have this beautiful body of work in a book.

I started making caramels in my Highland Park kitchen in 1999, after my first daughter was born and I'd retired from my job as a pastry chef. At home with a newborn, and freed from the demands of the pastry kitchen, I had time to play. Little did I know that it would turn into such an amazingly fun business. Thirteen years later, Little Flower is a café as well as a bakery and candy-making operation, and many stores across the nation carry our salty caramels.

I'm not a classically trained chef. I'm a baker who fell into making candy and, later, running a café. My recipes are simple and approachable. I love the imperfection of food, and my hope with this book is to encourage home cooks to join me in honoring this imperfection. The goal is not to create masterpieces. It's to have fun, keep it simple, keep it fresh, and don't overthink it. Make your cooking process enjoyable. Surround yourself with people who appreciate your efforts, then go for it. Play when you cook. And embrace the imperfections.

Most of all, cook with love. It is the most precious ingredient.

Gratefully,

Christine Moore

Eggs & Savory Tarts

The dishes in this chapter work equally well as cocktail party food and as main courses for brunch, lunch, or dinner. The secret is to make the Pâte Brisée Pie Shell and the Quick Puff Pastry in advance and have them both ready in your freezer. The chapter starts with those two staples, plus the Mustard Béchamel Sauce, since they're the foundations of many of the dishes that follow.

PÂTE BRISÉE PIE SHELL

Preparation time: 25 minutes plus 3 hours chilling time
Cooking time: 40 minutes
Makes two 9-inch pie shells

THIS RECIPE IS A MUST-HAVE IN YOUR REPERTOIRE. I USE IT FOR PIES AND QUICHES, BOTH SWEET AND SAVORY. HAVING A FEW DISKS OF THIS DOUGH IN YOUR FREEZER WILL MAKE IT EASY FOR YOU TO PULL SOMETHING TOGETHER QUICKLY AND BEAUTIFULLY. I SUGGEST FREEZING THE PIE SHELL WITH THE DOUGH ALREADY ROLLED OUT AND READY TO BAKE. JUST LET IT WARM UP FOR 15 MINUTES BEFORE BAKING.

3½ **cups all-purpose flour**
1 **teaspoon salt**
1½ **cups cold butter, cut into 1-inch cubes**
½ **cup cold water**

Mix flour and salt together in a large bowl. Cut the butter cubes into the flour by pinching them with your fingers or mixing with the paddle attachment of a stand mixer at low speed until the butter forms pea-size lumps. Add water all at once and mix until the dough just comes together into one mass. Divide dough in half. Form each into a flat disk by hand and wrap tightly in plastic. Chill thoroughly in the refrigerator for at least 2 hours.

When chilled, roll out each disk on a lightly floured surface to a 14-inch circle, ⅛ inch thick. Gently transfer to pie pan, making sure that the dough fully contacts the bottom and sides of the pan. Roll the dough overhang under itself and flute the edge. Chill thoroughly in the freezer for at least 1 hour before baking.

To bake the empty pie shells, preheat oven to 350°. If frozen, let sit on the counter for 15 minutes. Line each shell with parchment or paper coffee filters and fill with pie weights or dried beans. Bake until the crust under the paper appears dry and opaque, about 30 minutes. Remove weights and parchment and bake uncovered until crust starts to color, about 10 minutes.

QUICK PUFF PASTRY

Preparation time: 1 hour plus 2 hours chilling time
Cooking time: 30 minutes
Makes two 12 x 16-inch sheets

I HAVE THREE KIDS. KEEPING THINGS DOABLE AND SIMPLE IS THE ONLY WAY I ROLL. THIS QUICK PUFF PASTRY CAN BE WORKED INTO A SAVORY TART, A FRUIT TART, OR A BREAKFAST PASTRY. KEEP SOME ON HAND IN THE FREEZER FOR UNEXPECTED EVENTS—THERE'S NO THAWING TIME REQUIRED.

4 cups all-purpose flour
1½ teaspoons salt
3¼ cups cold butter, cut into 1-inch cubes
1 cup cold water

Combine flour and salt in a large bowl. Cut the butter cubes into the flour mixture by pinching them with your fingers or mixing on low speed with the paddle attachment of a stand mixer until the butter forms pea-size lumps. Add the water and mix until the dough just comes together. Shape into a flat disk, wrap in plastic wrap and chill for at least one hour in the refrigerator.

For the first turn, roll out the chilled dough on a lightly floured surface into a 28-inch x 16-inch x ¼-inch rectangle. Fold the dough into thirds like a letter. Wrap and chill for 15 minutes.

For the second turn, position the letter-folded rectangle so the seam side is facing you. Roll out, fold and chill as in the first turn. Repeat two more times. After completing the fourth turn, roll out the chilled dough once more into a 24-inch x 16-inch rectangle, omitting the letter-fold. Instead, cut the dough in half so you have two 12-inch x 16-inch rectangles. Prick each rectangle all over with a fork. Layer the pastry sheets on a single lined baking sheet, separating each layer with a parchment paper sheet. Wrap tightly in plastic and chill for at least 2 hours in the refrigerator. Can be made ahead and stored for up to 3 days in the refrigerator or 1 week in the freezer.

To bake for a savory tart, preheat oven to 375°. Place one thoroughly chilled (frozen is okay) 12-inch x 16-inch pastry rectangle on a baking sheet lined with parchment paper or a silicone mat. Bake until golden brown, approximately 30 minutes. If the pastry puffs during baking, flatten it with your mitted hand.

MUSTARD BÉCHAMEL SAUCE

Preparation time: 5 minutes
Cooking time: 6 minutes
Makes 1½ cups

BÉCHAMEL IS A WONDERFUL BINDER FOR SAVORY TARTS. ADDING WHOLE-GRAIN MUSTARD REALLY GIVES IT A SPECIAL KICK. IF YOU DON'T HAVE WHOLE GRAIN USE ANY REGULAR MUSTARD THAT YOU LOVE—OR EVEN A FLAVORED MUSTARD OR A PESTO.

---

1 tablespoon butter
1 tablespoon flour
1 cup milk
¼ teaspoon salt
2 tablespoons whole-grain mustard

Whisk the butter and flour in a small saucepan over medium-low heat and cook for a couple of minutes. Add the milk gradually, ¼ cup at a time, whisking thoroughly between additions to prevent lumps. Continue to stir with a whisk until the sauce comes to a slow boil and thickens, about 3 minutes. Take off heat and fold in the salt and mustard. Can be used immediately or stored in the refrigerator for up to one week.

Ham Tart

Preparation time: 20 minutes, plus Quick Puff Pastry and
Mustard Béchamel
Cooking time: 20 minutes, plus 30 minutes for Quick Puff Pastry
Makes 6 servings

I love French ham. It isn't as salty as domestic ham, and it has a silkier texture, if you can call ham silky. You can find it at Whole Foods and almost any gourmet market. Slice it as thinly as possible.

---

1 12 x 16-inch baked Quick Puff Pastry (see page 16)
½ cup Mustard Béchamel Sauce (see page 17)

Toppings:
8 ounces thinly sliced ham, French if possible
4 ounces thinly sliced Swiss cheese
½ cup chives, chopped

Preheat oven to 350°. Spread béchamel in a very thin layer over the baked puff pastry sheet. Arrange ham slices in a single layer over the béchamel, allowing it to fall in irregular ruffles like a dropped handkerchief. Place cheese slices in a single layer over the ham. Bake until the cheese and ham edges start to turn golden, about 20 minutes. Allow to cool slightly before slicing. Sprinkle with chives just before serving.

HEIRLOOM TOMATO & FETA TART

Preparation time: 25 minutes, plus Quick Puff Pastry and Mustard
Béchamel
Cooking time: 20 minutes, plus 30 minutes for Quick Puff Pastry
Makes 6 servings

THE COLLAGE OF COLORS AND TEXTURES IN THIS GORGEOUS TART MAKES IT
A TREAT FOR THE EYE AND THE TASTE BUDS.

½ cup Mustard Béchamel Sauce (see page 17)
1 12 x 16-inch baked Quick Puff Pastry
(see page 16)
2 heirloom tomatoes, sliced ¼-inch or thinner
(pieces okay)
½ cup crumbled feta cheese
1 tablespoon honey
½ cup roughly chopped flat-leaf parsley

Preheat oven to 350°. Spread béchamel in a very thin layer over the baked puff pastry sheet. Arrange tomato slices in a single layer, slightly overlapping. Sprinkle with crumbled feta and then drizzle honey evenly over the tart. Bake until the tomatoes and cheese start to turn golden, about 20 minutes. Allow to cool slightly before slicing. Sprinkle with parsley just before serving.

OLIVE & THYME TART

Preparation time: 20 minutes, plus Quick Puff Pastry
Cooking time: 15 minutes, plus 30 minutes for Quick Puff Pastry
Makes 6 servings

HERE IS A PERFECT EXAMPLE OF ADDING A DELICIOUS FLAVOR TO THE
BÉCHAMEL AND CREATING A YUMMY TART.

●───●

**¾ cup Olive Béchamel Sauce
(see recipe below)
1 12 x 16-inch baked Quick Puff Pastry
(see page 16)
2 teaspoons roughly chopped fresh
thyme leaves**

Preheat oven to 350°. Spread Olive Béchamel Sauce in a very thin
layer over the baked puff pastry sheet. Bake until the top starts to
turn golden, about 10 minutes. Allow to cool slightly before slicing.
With the long edge of the rectangle facing you, cut across the
pastry in a zigzag pattern for long triangle pieces. Sprinkle with
thyme just before serving.

Olive Béchamel Sauce

**1½ teaspoons butter
1½ teaspoons all-purpose flour
½ cup milk
½ cup Olive Tapenade (see Larder,
page 140)**

Whisk together butter and flour in a small saucepan over medium-
low heat and cook for a couple of minutes. Add the milk gradually,
¼ cup at a time, whisking thoroughly between additions to prevent
lumps. Continue to stir with a whisk until the sauce comes to a slow
boil and thickens, about 3 minutes. Remove from heat and stir in
Olive Tapenade.

ZUCCHINI & SPANISH GOAT CHEESE TART

Preparation time: 25 minutes, plus Quick Puff Pastry and
Mustard Béchamel Sauce
Cooking time: 20 minutes, plus 30 minutes for Quick Puff Pastry
Makes 6 servings

WHEN ZUCCHINI IS IN SEASON, THIS IS A WONDERFUL TART FOR A PARTY
BUFFET. MAKE SURE THE ZUCCHINI IS PAPER-THIN AND DRIZZLE SOME OLIVE
OIL ON IT BEFORE BAKING.

½ cup Mustard Béchamel Sauce (see
    page 17)
1 12 x 16-inch baked Quick Puff Pastry (see
    page 16)
2 large zucchini, sliced paper-thin with a
    mandoline or food processor
1 tablespoon olive oil
8 ounces ripened goat cheese, sliced into
    ¼-inch rounds or crumbled if soft
½ cup chopped chives

Preheat oven to 350°. Spread béchamel in a very thin layer over
the baked puff pastry sheet. Toss the zucchini in the olive oil and
arrange in a single layer, slightly overlapping. Place goat cheese
on top. Bake until the zucchini and cheese start to turn golden,
about 20 minutes. Allow to cool slightly before slicing. Sprinkle with
chives just before serving.

QUICHE WITH LEEKS & DIJON

Preparation time: 10 minutes, plus Pâte Brisée Pie Shell and Melted Leeks
Cooking time: 50-60 minutes, plus 40 minutes for Pie Shell
Makes one 9-inch pie, 8-10 servings

MUSTARD AND LEEKS MAKE A SUPERB FLAVOR COMBINATION. BRINGING
THEM TOGETHER IN A QUICHE MIGHT SOUND ODD, BUT IT PROVIDES A DEPTH
OF FLAVOR THAT WILL SURPRISE YOU—IN A REALLY GOOD WAY.

●━━━━━━━━━━━━━━━━━━━━━━━━━━━━●

6 large eggs
1 cup milk
⅔ cup cream
3 generous tablespoons Dijon mustard
½ teaspoon salt
1 pinch ground white pepper
1 cup grated Swiss cheese
½ cup Melted Leeks (see Larder, page 139)
1 tablespoon chopped fresh tarragon
1 baked Pâte Brisée Pie Shell (see page 15)

Preheat oven to 350°. Whisk together eggs, milk, cream, mustard,
salt, and pepper. Strain by pouring custard through a sieve into a
bowl. Stir cheese, leeks, and tarragon into the strained custard.
Pour into the baked shell. Place pie dish on a baking sheet before
placing in oven. Bake until eggs set, 50 to 60 minutes. Insert a
small paring knife in the middle of the quiche to ensure that the
custard is set and no longer liquid.

Quiche with Sautéed Mushrooms, Goat Cheese & Thyme

Preparation time: 10 minutes, plus Pâte Brisée Pie Shell and
Sautéed Mushrooms
Cooking time: 45 minutes, plus 40 minutes for Pie Shell
Makes one 9-inch pie, 8 servings

I love the earthy combination of mushrooms and goat cheese together, so I love this quiche. And so do my customers.

6 large eggs
1 cup milk
⅔ cup cream
½ teaspoon salt
1 pinch ground white pepper
½ cup Sautéed Mushrooms (see Larder, page 140)
¼ cup coarsely crumbled goat cheese
1 teaspoon chopped fresh thyme leaves
1 baked Pâte Brisée Pie Shell (see page 15)

Preheat oven to 350°. Whisk together eggs, milk, cream, salt, and pepper. Pour custard through a fine sieve into a bowl. Add Sautéed Mushrooms, goat cheese, and thyme to the strained custard. Pour custard into the baked pie shell. Place pie dish on a baking sheet and bake until set, 40 to 45 minutes. Insert a small paring knife in the middle of the quiche to ensure that the custard is set and no longer liquid.

EGG TERRINE

Preparation time: 15 minutes, plus Larder Ingredients
Cooking time: 1 hour 15 minutes
Makes 8 servings

THIS IS GREAT FOR A BREAKFAST PARTY. SLICE AND SERVE WARM OR ROOM TEMP WITH A SALAD OR SWEET FRUIT. IT LOOKS IMPRESSIVE TOO!

●───●

½ of a red tomato, thinly sliced
1 pinch salt
2 tablespoon butter, room temperature
14 large eggs
1¼ cups grated Cheddar cheese
½ cup fresh whole tarragon leaves
½ cup Tomato Confit (see Larder, page 141)
15-20 Roasted Asparagus spears (see Larder, page 140)
¼ cup grated carrot

Preheat oven to 350°. Heat a kettle-full of water to boiling and set aside. Sprinkle the salt over the sliced tomato and set aside. Grease a 9 x 5-inch loaf pan with the butter, being especially liberal in all the corners of the pan. Gently crack 4 eggs in the bottom of the pan so the yolks stay intact. Arrange in single layers ½ cup of cheese, ½ cup of Tomato Confit, and ¼ cup tarragon. Crack another 4 eggs on top. Arrange in single layers ½ cup of cheese, all the asparagus spears and ¼ cup tarragon. For the final egg layer, use 6 eggs. Sprinkle on top in single layers ¼ cup cheese and ¼ cup carrot. Dab the reserved tomato slices dry with a kitchen towel and arrange across the top of the terrine without overlapping. Cover tightly in aluminum foil.

To bake, place a 8 x 11-inch rectangular casserole dish in the middle of the oven. Fill halfway with the hot water. Place the covered terrine in the middle of the hot water bath and bake for 1 hour. Remove the foil cover and bake until the egg completely sets and the top turns golden, about 15 to 20 minutes. Check by inserting a sharp knife down the center of the terrine. Allow to cool 10 minutes. Unmold the terrine by placing a large plate across the top of the pan and flipping it upside down. Remove the pan by easing it straight upwards, then invert the terrine back onto a serving plate so the tomato layer is back on top.

BAKED EGGS WITH SPINACH

Preparation time: 5 minutes, plus Sautéed Spinach
Cooking time: 10-15 minutes
Makes 1 serving

EGGS ARE A PERFECT FOOD. ESPECIALLY THE FRESH ONES FROM MY FRIEND
SARA. THIS IS A SIMPLE WAY TO CELEBRATE THEIR BEAUTY, AND IF YOU CAN
GET THEM FROM A FARMERS' MARKET OR A FRIEND, SO MUCH THE BETTER.
IF YOU DON'T HAVE SPINACH, USE ANY TENDER GREEN IN SEASON.

——

**3 tablespoons Sautéed Spinach (see Larder,
page 141)**
3 eggs
2 tablespoons herb bread crumbs

Preheat oven to 350°. Generously butter an 8-ounce capacity gratin
dish. Place the spinach in a single layer on the bottom of the dish.
Crack the eggs over the spinach and sprinkle with bread crumbs.
Bake until the eggs set, 12 to 15 minutes, depending on your
preference.

BAKED OLIVES

Preparation time: 10 minutes
Cooking time: 25 minutes
Makes 10-12 servings

FUN AND EASY! I KEEP A BIG JAR OF THESE IN THE FRIDGE, AND WHEN FRIENDS COME OVER, I SPOON SOME INTO A LITTLE CAST-IRON POT. A WARM AND SALTY TREAT WITH A COCKTAIL.

½ cup pearl onions
1 cup oil-cured black olives (any variety)
1 cup green olives (I use French Lucques,
   but any kind is fine)
½ cup whole garlic cloves, peeled
Peel of 1 orange
Peel of 1 lemon
2 sprigs fresh thyme
1 cup olive oil

Preheat oven to 350⁰. Place the pearl onions, skin on, in a small pot of boiling water for 2 to 3 minutes. Drain and cool slightly. Remove the peels, which should slip right off.

Toss the peeled onions and all the remaining ingredients together in a gratin dish. (Or, if you're assembling ahead, in a jar or bowl to store in the fridge.) Bake, uncovered, until oil starts bubbling, approximately 20 minutes. Serve warm with crusty bread, and don't forget to put out a small dish for the pits!

BAKERY

Baking is at the very heart of the Little Flower kitchen. The recipes here are daily favorites: some as breakfast treats to have with coffee, others to serve alongside a lunch or dinner entree. Each is an essential staple in my kitchen.

—————————•————————————————•—————————

BAKERY

Baking is at the very heart of the Little Flower kitchen. The recipes here are daily favorites: some as breakfast treats to have with coffee, others to serve alongside a lunch or dinner entree. Each is an essential staple in my kitchen.

BLUEBERRY MUFFINS

Preparation time: 30 minutes
Cooking time: 20-25 minutes
Makes 12 servings

WE ACTUALLY TRIED TO TAKE THIS OFF THE MENU WHEN BLUEBERRY
SEASON WAS OVER. BIG MISTAKE. NOW WE SUBSTITUTE FROZEN
BLUEBERRIES THE REST OF THE YEAR.

¾ cup plus 2 tablespoons sugar, divided
2 large eggs, separated
½ cup butter at room temperature
1 teaspoon vanilla extract
1¼ cups cake flour
¾ teaspoon baking powder
¼ teaspoon salt
½ cup milk
¾ cup frozen blueberries
1 teaspoon flour (cake or all-purpose)
Confectioner's sugar for dusting

Preheat oven to 350°. Line tins of cupcake pan with paper liners.
Using an electric mixer, whip the egg whites with ½ cup of the
sugar at high speed until the peaks are stiff and glossy. Set aside.

In a separate large bowl, beat together the butter and remaining
sugar until pale. Add the egg yolks and vanilla to the butter mixture,
scraping down sides of bowl a couple of times during mixing.

In a third bowl, combine flour, baking powder, and salt. At low
speed, add one third of the flour mixture into the butter-yolk
mixture, then half the milk. Scrape down the sides of the bowl.
Repeat. Then mix in the last third of the flour mixture and gently
fold in the whipped egg whites until just combined.

Scoop batter into prepared cupcake tins, filling ¾ full. Toss the
frozen blueberries in the teaspoon of flour to coat. Shake off any
excess and place a generous pinch of blueberries on top of each
muffin. The berries will settle into the muffin on their own during
baking. Bake until toothpick inserted in the middle of the cake
comes out clean, about 25 minutes. Dust with confectioner's sugar
when completely cooled.

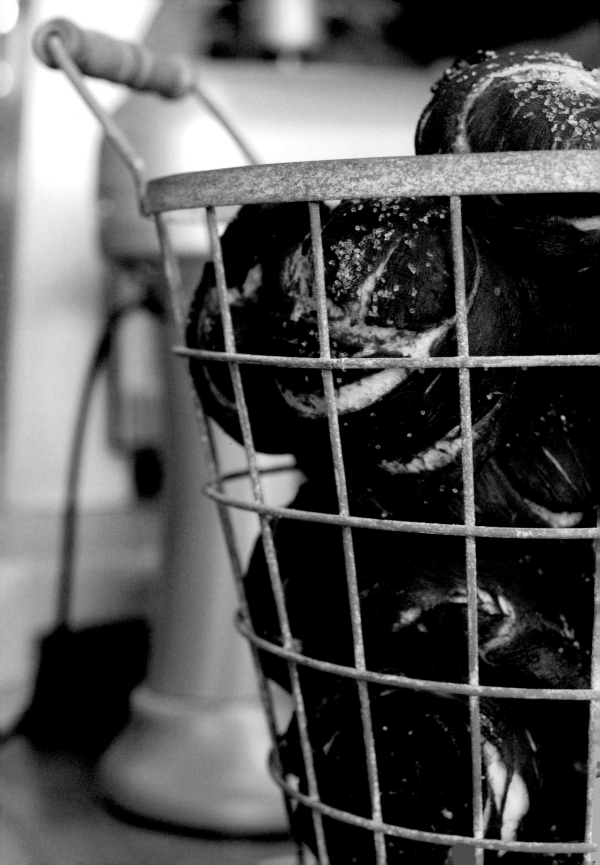

BUTTERMILK PRETZEL ROLLS

Preparation time: 30 minutes, plus 1 hour rest
Cooking time: 25 minutes, plus 5 minutes poaching time
Makes 16 servings

I GREW UP IN NEW JERSEY. ON WEEKENDS, WE'D TRAVEL INTO NEW YORK CITY FOR MUSEUM VISITS AND CENTRAL PARK. WE ALWAYS GOT A WARM, SOFT PRETZEL FROM A STREET CART, AND I CAN STILL SMELL THE ROASTING CHESTNUTS FROM THE VENDORS. THE SMELLS AND MEMORIES FROM CHILDHOOD ARE SO POWERFUL AND COMFORTING. MAKING THESE PRETZEL ROLLS EVERY DAY IN THE CAFÉ KEEPS THOSE MEMORIES ALIVE.

2 tablespoons active dry yeast
1½ cups warm water
½ cup plus 2 tablespoons buttermilk*
2 tablespoons and 1 teaspoon extra-light olive oil, divided
5 cups bread flour
⅓ cup firmly packed light brown sugar
2 teaspoons granulated sugar
1 tablespoon salt

For poaching liquid:
6 tablespoons baking soda
1 cup firmly packed light brown sugar
3 cups water

For garnish:
⅓ cup oil
2 tablespoons kosher salt

Dissolve yeast in warm water and set aside until foamy, about 5 minutes. Add buttermilk and 2 tablespoons of oil. Set wet mixture aside. Combine flour, sugars, and salt in the large bowl of a stand mixer. Add wet mixture all at once. Mix with a dough hook on medium-low speed until the dough is smooth and tacky, about 15 minutes. Lightly coat the dough mass with the remaining teaspoon of oil. Cover loosely with plastic wrap and allow the dough to rise at room temperature until it doubles in volume, about 1 hour.

Line 2 baking sheets with parchment paper or silicone mats. Brush the paper with oil. After it has risen, turn the dough onto a lightly floured surface. Cut the dough into tennis ball–size mounds. Roll each mound into a 6-inch rope and then tie into a simple knot. Divide the knots between the prepared baking sheets.

Preheat oven to 350°. For poaching liquid, mix baking soda, brown sugar, and water in a large saucepan. Heat to a gentle boil, adjusting heat as necessary so the poaching liquid doesn't boil over. Using a slotted spoon, submerge the knots three at a time into the hot poaching liquid for 8 seconds on each side. Return to lined baking sheets and brush with oil and sprinkle with a pinch of kosher salt. Bake until the rolls turn a nice amber brown, about 25 minutes, rotating baking sheets halfway through.

If you do not have buttermilk, combine ⅔ cup milk with 2 teaspoons of lemon juice. Set aside until the milk curdles, about 2 minutes.

CINNAMON ROLLS

Preparation time: 30 minutes, plus 1¼ hour chilling time
Cooking time: 25 minutes, plus 30 minutes for Quick Puff Pastry
Makes 8 servings

NOT YOUR TRADITIONAL CINNAMON ROLL, THESE BAKE UP CRISP,
FLAKY, AND BUTTERY. MAKE SURE YOU COOK THEM ALL THE WAY TO A
DARK GOLDEN BROWN.

½ **recipe Quick Puff Pastry, thawed if**
   frozen (see page 16)
½ **cup butter**
1 **cup firmly packed light brown sugar**
1 **tablespoon ground cinnamon**
¼ **teaspoon salt**
1 **tablespoon egg white**
½ **cup chopped pecans**

Preheat oven to 350°. To make the filling, beat together the butter, sugar, cinnamon, and salt, starting on low speed to avoid a cloud of cinnamon dust. Once the cinnamon has been incorporated, increase to high and beat until the mixture is pale in color. Add egg white and continue to beat on high until light and fluffy. Set aside at room temperature.

Roll out the chilled (but thawed) quick puff pastry dough on a lightly floured surface into a 16-inch x18-inch x ⅛-inch rectangle. Place on a baking sheet lined with parchment paper or a silicone mat and chill thoroughly in the freezer for at least 15 minutes. Spread 1 cup of the cinnamon filling on top of the chilled pastry sheet in a thin, even layer, using an offset spatula or bench knife. Scrape off excess. Spread chopped pecans evenly over the filling. Take the short edge of the rectangle and roll the pastry into a tight log. Allow the roll to firm up in the freezer for at least 45 minutes. Once chilled, cut into 8 even slices. Return to the freezer and thoroughly chill for at least 20 minutes before baking. Can store for up to a month in the freezer.

To bake, arrange frozen rolls cut side facing up on the lined baking sheet. Bake until golden and the center is cooked through, about 25 minutes.

GRANOLA

Preparation time: 20 minutes
Cooking time: 30 minutes
Makes 16 servings (8 cups)

MY MOM MADE GRANOLA FOR US AS KIDS GROWING UP IN NEW JERSEY IN
THE 1960S. ALL WE WANTED WAS CAP'N CRUNCH. THANKS, MOM, FOR
ALWAYS BEING ON THE CUTTING EDGE—AND FOR TAKING US TO WOODSTOCK.

½ cup extra-light olive oil
½ cup brown sugar
½ cup real maple syrup
1 tablespoon vanilla extract
½ teaspoon salt
4 cups old-fashioned rolled oats
1 cup sliced almonds
1 cup chopped pecans
1 cup pepitas (pumpkin seeds)
1 cup sweetened flaked coconut
1 cup dried cranberries
1 cup chopped dried apples or pears
1 cup chopped dried apricots

Preheat oven to 325°. Line two baking sheets with parchment
paper or silicone mats. In a saucepan, heat oil, sugar, maple
syrup, vanilla, and salt over medium-low heat until sugar dissolves.
Remove from heat and set aside. In a separate bowl, use your
hands to combine oats, nuts, seeds, and coconut. Pour the wet
mixture over oats mixture and mix until thoroughly combined. Divide
the granola between the two baking sheets and spread into a single
layer. Bake until golden, about 30 minutes, stirring and rotating the
pans every 10 minutes. Once cooled, mix in dried fruits.

LEMON - GINGER SCONES

Preparation time: 20 minutes, plus 1 hour chilling time
Cooking time: 30-35 minutes
Makes 15 servings

THESE SCONES ARE BUTTERY, CRUMBLY, AND MELT-IN-YOUR-MOUTH GOOD.
DON'T OVERMIX THEM—JUST GET THE DOUGH TO COME TOGETHER, AND LET
THE OVEN DO THE REST.

5 cups cake flour
½ cup sugar
2 teaspoons salt
2 tablespoons baking powder
1½ cups cold butter, cut into 1-inch
   cubes
1 cup candied ginger, chopped
3 tablespoons lemon zest
1 cup heavy cream, divided
1 egg
⅓ cup sugar for sprinkling

Combine flour, sugar, salt, and baking powder. Cut the butter cubes
into the flour mixture by pinching them with your fingers or mixing
with the paddle attachment of a stand mixer at low speed until the
butter forms pea-size lumps. Add the ginger and lemon zest. Stir
in ¾ cup cream until the dough just comes together. In a separate
bowl, beat together egg and remaining ¼ cup cream and set aside.
Form the dough into imperfect mounds roughly the size of a tennis
ball by pressing the dough between cupped hands. Arrange on
a baking sheet lined with parchment paper or a silicone mat and
brush the surfaces with egg-cream wash. Chill thoroughly in freezer
for at least 1 hour. Can store for up to a month in freezer.

Preheat oven to 350°. Sprinkle the frozen scones with a very
generous pinch of sugar before placing in the oven. Bake scones
until golden, 30 to 35 minutes.

Variation: Orange-Cranberry Scones

Replace ginger and lemon zest with 1½ cups dried cranberries and
2 tablespoons orange zest.

MUSHROOM BISCUITS

Preparation time: 25 minutes, plus 1 hour chilling time
Cooking time: 35 minutes
Makes 16 servings

THESE BISCUITS SATISFY THE SAVORY MORNING CRAVING—AND THEY'RE ALSO
DELICIOUS WITH A SALAD AND SOUP FOR DINNER.

●━━━━━━━━━━━━━━━━━━━━━━━━━━━━━━●

4¼ cups all-purpose flour
4 teaspoons baking powder
2 teaspoons salt
1½ cups cold butter, cut into 1-inch cubes
1½ cups Sautéed Mushrooms (see Larder,
   page 140)
1½ cups Swiss cheese, grated
½ cup coarsely chopped parsley
4 large eggs
1 cup heavy cream

Combine flour, baking powder, and salt. Cut the butter cubes into
the flour mixture by pinching them with your fingers or mixing with
the paddle attachment of a stand mixer at low speed until the
butter forms pea-size lumps. Add the Sautéed Mushrooms, cheese,
and parsley. In a separate bowl, beat together eggs and cream.
Combine the egg and flour mixtures until the dough just comes
together. Turn the dough out onto a lightly floured surface and
gently shape into a rough 10 x 10 x 1½-inch square. Cut into 16
squares. Chill thoroughly in the freezer for at least 1 hour. Can store
for up to a month in the freezer.

Preheat oven to 350°. Remove from freezer, place on a baking
sheet lined with parchment paper or a silicone mat, and bake until
golden, about 35 minutes.

Variation: Bacon, Cheddar & Chive Biscuits

Replace mushrooms, Swiss cheese, and parsley with 1½ cups
coarsely chopped bacon, 1½ cups shredded cheddar cheese,
½ cup chopped fresh chives, and 1 teaspoon onion powder.

OATCAKES

Preparation time: 20 minutes
Cooking time: 25-30 minutes
Makes 12 servings

OATY AND TENDER, WITH A HINT OF SWEETNESS, THESE ARE ALWAYS AT THE
READY IN MY FREEZER TO BAKE UP ON CRISP WINTER MORNINGS. I LOVE
THESE CAKES.

3 cups old-fashioned rolled oats, plus 1
   tablespoon for sprinkling
¾ cup grated carrot
2¼ cups all-purpose flour
¾ cup cornmeal
¼ cup plus 2 tablespoons firmly packed
   light brown sugar
2¼ teaspoons baking soda
2 teaspoons salt
1½ cups cold butter, cut into 1-inch cubes
¾ cup buttermilk
1 cup honey
¾ cup raisins
¼ cup plus 2 tablespoons flaxseed

Preheat oven to 350°. Grease cupcake tins with butter or cooking
spray. Put oats and shredded carrot in a food processor and grind
into a coarse meal. In a large bowl, mix together flour, cornmeal,
sugar, baking soda, salt, and oat-carrot mixture. Cut the butter
cubes into the flour mixture by pinching them with your fingers or
mixing with the paddle attachment of a stand mixer at low speed
until the butter forms pea-size lumps. Fold in the buttermilk, honey,
raisins, and flax until the dough just comes together.

Divide the dough evenly between the 12 tins of the cupcake pan,
mounding each high and tall. Gently press a few rolled oats onto
the top of each mound. Bake until golden brown, 25 to 30 minutes.

SALADS & DRESSINGS

Fresh and simple, with clear flavors—that's how I like my salads. And that's exactly what you'll find in the recipes in this chapter.

CARROT GINGER DRESSING

Preparation time: 10 minutes
Makes 2½ cups

1 shallot, peeled
2 cloves garlic, peeled
3 tablespoons fresh ginger, peeled
   (about a 3-inch knob)
½ cup carrot, grated (1 medium carrot)
½ teaspoon ground mustard
2 teaspoons soy sauce
½ cup seasoned rice wine vinegar
1 teaspoon toasted sesame oil
¾ cup canola oil
¼ cup extra-virgin olive oil
Salt to taste

Roughly chop the shallot, garlic, and ginger and toss into a wide glass or small bowl. Add the carrot, mustard, soy, vinegar, and oils. Puree with an immersion blender until smooth. Add salt to taste. Store in an airtight container in the refrigerator for up to 1 week.

Make-Ahead Variation

Alternatively, finely chop the shallot and garlic and grate the ginger by hand. Combine with the carrot, mustard, soy, and vinegar. Slowly stream in the oils, whisking constantly with a hand whisk. Salt to taste. Store dressing in an airtight container in the refrigerator for up to 1 week.

LEMON THYME DRESSING

Preparation time: 10 minutes
Makes 4 cups

---

1 shallot, peeled
1 clove garlic, peeled
1½ teaspoons Dijon mustard
½ cup apple cider vinegar
½ cup lemon juice
1 tablespoon fresh thyme leaves
½ teaspoon salt
2 cups canola oil
1 cup extra-virgin olive oil

Finely chop the shallot and garlic. Combine in a small bowl with the mustard, vinegar, lemon juice, thyme, and salt. Slowly stream in the oils, whisking constantly. Taste and add salt if necessary. Store in an airtight container in the refrigerator for up to 1 week.

RED WINE VINAIGRETTE

Preparation time: 10 minutes
Makes 4 cups

---

1 shallot, finely diced
1 clove garlic, minced
1½ teaspoons Dijon mustard
1 cup red wine vinegar
2 cups canola oil
1 cup extra-virgin olive oil
½ teaspoon salt

Combine shallot and garlic in a small bowl with the mustard, vinegar, and salt. Slowly stream in the oils, whisking constantly. Taste and add salt if necessary. Store in an airtight container in the refrigerator for up to 1 week.

SHERRY VINAIGRETTE

Preparation time: 10 minutes
Makes 4 cups

1 shallot, peeled
1 clove garlic, peeled
1½ teaspoons Dijon mustard
1 cup sherry vinegar
½ teaspoon salt 2 cups canola oil
1 cup extra-virgin olive oil

Finely chop the shallot and garlic. Combine in a small bowl with the mustard, vinegar, and salt. Slowly stream in the oils, whisking constantly. Taste and add salt if necessary. Store in an airtight container in the refrigerator for up to 1 week.

VIETNAMESE DRESSING

Preparation time: 5 minutes
Makes 1½ cups

⅓ cup plus 1 tablespoon rice wine vinegar
¼ cup Maggi Seasoning Sauce
2 tablespoons sugar
¾ cup canola oil
¼ cup extra-virgin olive oil
Salt to taste

Whisk together vinegar, Maggi, and sugar in a small bowl until sugar dissolves. Slowly stream in the oils, whisking constantly. Salt to taste. Store dressing in an airtight container in the refrigerator for up to 1 week.

Barley, Wheat Berries, Red Quinoa, and Herb Salad

Preparation time: 5 minutes, plus Cooked Grains and Sherry Vinaigrette
Makes 8-10 servings

THIS DELICIOUS SALAD TAKES A LITTLE WORK BECAUSE IT HAS FOUR DIFFERENT COOKED GRAINS, BUT THE COMBINATION OF TEXTURES AND FLAVORS MAKES IT WELL WORTH IT—PLUS YOU CAN COOK THE GRAINS IN ADVANCE.

1 cup cooked barley (see Larder, page 138)
1 cup cooked red quinoa (see Larder, page 140)
1 cup cooked wheat berries (see Larder, page 141)
1 cup cooked bulgur (see Larder, page 139)
½ cup chopped fresh mint
½ cup chopped fresh dill
½ cup chopped fresh basil
¼ cup chopped chives
½ cup Sherry Vinaigrette (see page 57)
Salt to taste

In a large serving bowl, toss the cooked grains with the fresh herbs and vinaigrette. Salt to taste.

CURRIED CHICKEN SALAD

Preparation time: 30 minutes, plus Apricot Chutney and Sherry Vinaigrette
Cooking time: 20-30 minutes
Makes 1 meal-size salad, with extra chicken left over

I CAN'T LOOK AT CURRY WITHOUT REMEMBERING THE NIGHT MY MOTHER PUT CURRY POWDER IN THE TUNA NOODLE CASSEROLE. I THINK WE ALL WENT TO BED HUNGRY.

Curried Chicken:
4 boneless chicken breasts
    (about 2 pounds)
Salt and pepper to taste
¼ cup lemon juice
½ cup yellow curry powder
1 cup sliced almonds
1½ cups mayonnaise
1 cup plain yogurt
1 tablespoon plus 1½ teaspoons
    honey
¼ cup lemon juice
¼ cup yellow curry powder
¼ cup turmeric

2 cups red grapes, halved
½ onion, finely diced
Salt and pepper to taste

Salad:
3 cups mixed greens, firmly
    packed
2 tablespoons Sherry
Vinaigrette (see page 57)
⅔ cup Curried Chicken
2 tablespoons Apricot
    Chutney (see Larder, page
    138)
2 tablespoons toasted
    almonds

Season the chicken generously with salt and pepper. Combine in a bowl with lemon juice and curry. Set aside for 10 minutes. Preheat oven to 350°. Bake the chicken until cooked through, 20 to 30 minutes. While the chicken is cooking, spread the sliced almonds in a single layer on a separate baking sheet. Bake in the same oven until they turn golden, 8 to 10 minutes.

When cool enough to handle, cube the chicken into bite-size pieces. In a large bowl, combine the chicken and almonds with the mayonnaise, yogurt, honey, lemon juice, curry, turmeric, grapes, and onion. Add salt and pepper to taste.

Toss the greens with the vinaigrette in a serving bowl. Arrange the chicken and apricot chutney side by side on top. Sprinkle with 2 tablespoons toasted almonds before serving.

FRESH PEAS & PANCETTA SALAD

Preparation time: 15 minutes
Cooking time: 5 minutes
Makes 4 servings

I LOVE TO MAKE THIS SALAD IN EARLY SPRING BECAUSE MY KIDS DEVOUR IT. THE ARUGULA IS NUTTY AND YOUNG, AND THE SPRING PEAS ARE SWEET.

——————————————————————————————

1 cup fresh peas (or frozen)
½ cup pancetta, cut into ¼-inch cubes
1 avocado
Fresh lemon juice
¼ cup red wine vinegar
¼ cup extra-virgin olive oil
¼ teaspoon salt
4 cups firmly packed arugula leaves
⅓ cup Parmesan, shaved
Ground black pepper to taste

Bring 1 quart of water to a rolling boil. Blanch the peas for 2 minutes and drain. Set aside to cool.

Brown the pancetta in a sauté pan and set aside. Halve the avocado, remove the pit, thinly slice the flesh, and scoop it out with a soup spoon. Sprinkle with some lemon juice and set aside. Whisk together vinegar, olive oil, and salt. Dress the arugula to taste. Top the greens with the peas, pancetta, avocado, Parmesan, and black pepper to taste.

GODDESS SALAD

Preparation time: 10 minutes, plus Larder Ingredients and
Lemon Thyme Dressing
Makes 1 meal-size serving

MY DEAR FRIEND GLENYS HAS BEEN KNOWN TO DRIVE FROM SAN
FRANCISCO TO LOS ANGELES AND GO STRAIGHT INTO THE KITCHEN TO
COOK FOR MY FAMILY. FOR A PROFESSIONAL COOK, IT'S AN INCREDIBLE
TREAT TO HAVE SOMEONE COOK FOR YOU. ONCE SHE MADE A DELICIOUS
SALAD WITH GRATED EGG AND HARICOTS VERTS. HERE'S MY VERSION.

——

**20 Blanched French Green Beans (see
Larder, page 138)**
**⅓ cup Hard-boiled Egg, chopped (see
Larder, page 139)**
**2 tablespoons Lemon Thyme Dressing
(see page 56)**
**3 cups hand-torn butter lettuce leaves,
firmly packed**
½ cup cucumber, cut in ¼-inch slices
¼ cup feta, crumbled
1 tablespoon chives, minced

Toss the lettuce in the dressing and place in a serving bowl.
Arrange the cucumber, green beans, egg, and feta on top of the
lettuce in distinct sections. Sprinkle with chives before serving.

HERB SALAD

Preparation time: 15 minutes, plus Lemon Thyme Dressing
Makes 1 meal-size serving

THIS SALAD IS SPECIAL! IT SOUNDS SIMPLE, BUT THE FRESH HERBS ARE SO COMPLEMENTARY AND MAKE SUCH A VIBRANT FLAVOR COMBINATION. IT'S PERFECT WITH THE LIGHT LEMON THYME DRESSING, OR EVEN JUST WITH LEMON JUICE, OLIVE OIL, AND SALT.

1 cup mixed greens, firmly packed
1 cup butter lettuce leaves, firmly packed
1 cup arugula, firmly packed
¼ cup flat-leaf parsley leaves
¼ cup basil leaves, torn
¼ cup mint leaves
¼ cup fresh dill, stemmed
¼ cup fresh tarragon, stemmed
1 tablespoon chives, chopped
2 tablespoons Lemon Thyme Dressing
   (see page 56)

Combine the lettuces and herbs in a serving bowl. Toss the greens with the dressing.

VIETNAMESE SALAD WITH BAKED TOFU

Preparation time: 15 minutes plus Baked Tofu and Vietnamese Dressing
Makes 1 meal-size serving

3 cups firmly packed mixed greens
2 tablespoon plus 1 teaspoon Vietnamese
   Dressing, divided (see page 57)
2 tablespoons julienned carrot
2 tablespoons julienned daikon radish
2 tablespoons thinly sliced red onion
⅓ cup thinly sliced Persian cucumbers
9 ¼-inch slices Baked Tofu (see Larder,
   page 138)
2 tablespoons thinly sliced jalapeño
¼ cup cilantro leaves

Toss the greens with 2 tablespoons of Vietnamese Dressing. Top the greens with the carrot, daikon, onion, cucumbers, tofu, jalapeño, and cilantro. Sprinkle the salad with the remaining dressing.

Sandwiches & Bowls

I love a good sandwich. Growing up in New Jersey in the '70s, I fell early for what we Jersey kids called subs—hearty sandwiches oozing with oil , red wine vinegar, and dried oregano. I can still smell the campus sub shop at Seton Hall University, not to mention the Town Hall Deli, which is famous for its sloppy joe sandwich: a dry slaw, ham, turkey, and Swiss concoction that I will crave until I die. It's true: A well-constructed sandwich is a work of art.

BROWN RICE BOWL

Preparation time: 5 minutes, plus Larder Ingredients and
Carrot Ginger Dressing
Makes 1 meal-size serving

THIS IS THE SINGLE MOST POPULAR DISH AT THE CAFÉ. I CREATED IT
BECAUSE IT'S WHAT I WANTED TO EAT FOR LUNCH EVERY DAY: A NOURISHING
AND DELICIOUS MEAL OF WARM BROWN RICE, FRESH VEGETABLES, AND
TOFU.

1 ½ cups cooked Brown Rice
(see Larder, page 139)
10 Blanched French Green Beans
(see Larder, page 138)
¼ cup cooked Black-eyed Peas
(see Larder, page 138)
¼ cup Sautéed Mushrooms
(see Larder, page 140)
4 ¼-inch slices Baked Tofu
(see Larder, page 138)
¼ red bell pepper, sliced into matchsticks
¼ cup shredded carrot
⅓ cup Carrot Ginger Dressing
(see page 55)
1 tablespoon black and white
sesame seeds, mixed
1 tablespoon nori, cut into ¼-inch strips
(use scissors)
1 tablespoon microgreens

If you don't have rice prepared, cook up a fresh batch. If you have
some ready in the refrigerator, reheat by placing in a baking dish
or heatproof bowl, sprinkling with water, covering with foil, and
warming in a 300° oven until steamy warm, about 10 minutes.

Scoop warm brown rice into a serving bowl. Arrange the green
beans, black-eyed peas, mushrooms, tofu, red bell pepper, and
carrot on top of the rice in distinct sections. Drizzle with dressing.
Sprinkle sesame seeds, nori, and microgreens in successive layers
over the middle of the bowl.

BRIE & MUSHROOM SANDWICH

Preparation time: 10 minutes, plus Sautéed Mushrooms
Makes 1 serving

EARTHY MUSHROOMS, CREAMY MELTING CHEESE, AND ZESTY LEMON MAKE
THIS A FAVORITE AT THE CAFÉ. YOU CAN ALSO PLACE THE SAME TOPPINGS
ON BREAD ROUNDS TO MAKE A TERRIFIC APPETIZER.

¼ baguette, halved lengthwise
½ cup Sautéed Mushrooms
    (see Larder, page 140)
2 ounces brie, cut into 6 slices
Zest of one lemon
1½ teaspoons fresh thyme leaves

Preheat oven to 350°. Place baguette halves side by side on a
baking pan, cut side up. Spread the mushrooms across both slices
of bread. Arrange brie in a single layer over the mushrooms. Bake
until the cheese melts and the bread crisps, about 5 minutes.
Sprinkle with lemon zest and thyme.

BROCCOLINI & BURRATA SANDWICH

Preparation time: 5 minutes, plus Roasted Broccolini and
Tomato Confit
Makes 1 serving

BURRATA, BURRATA, BURRATA! ADDING BROCCOLINI TO THIS AMAZING
CHEESE SANDWICH WILL ASSUAGE YOUR GUILT.

⎯⎯⎯⎯⎯⎯⎯⎯⎯⎯⎯⎯⎯⎯⎯⎯⎯⎯⎯⎯⎯⎯⎯⎯⎯⎯⎯⎯⎯⎯⎯

**7 Roasted Broccolini
(see Larder, page 140)
⅓ cup Tomato Confit
(see Larder, page 141)
⅓ ciabatta loaf, halved lengthwise
1 tablespoon olive oil
⅓ cup burrata, sliced**

Drizzle the bread with olive oil. Arrange the broccolini in a single
layer on the bottom half, followed by the burrata and then the
tomato confit. Top with the other slice of bread.

Party Variation
For an appetizer course at a party, use an entire ciabatta loaf sliced
in half, 1 whole bunch Roasted Broccolini, 1 cup Tomato Confit,
1 cup sliced burrata, and 3 tablespoons olive oil. Assemble as
directed above and slice into small strips.

CURRIED CHICKEN SANDWICH

Preparation time: 5 minutes, plus Curried Chicken and Apricot Chutney
Makes 1 serving

ON A CHEWY CIABATTA BREAD, THE COMBINATION OF SWEET CHUTNEY AND
SAVORY CHICKEN SALAD REALLY SATISFIES. WE USE BREAD FROM SUMI
CHANG AT PASADENA'S EURO PANE BECAUSE IT'S THE ABSOLUTE BEST, BUT
ANY GOOD CIABATTA WILL MAKE YOU HAPPY.

⅓ ciabatta loaf, halved lengthwise
⅔ cup Curried Chicken (see page 61)
1 tablespoon sliced almonds, toasted
2 romaine leaves
1 generous tablespoon Apricot Chutney
(see Larder, page 138)

Place Curried Chicken on the bottom half of bread. Sprinkle the
chicken with almonds and then cover with romaine leaves. Slather
chutney on the other half of bread and place on top.

GREEN TURKEY SANDWICH

Preparation time: 10 minutes, plus Aioli and Edamame Spread
Makes 1 serving

CREATED BY THE TIRELESS KATIE MCNEIL, THIS VERY
GREEN DELIGHT IS A BESTSELLER.

---

2 teaspoons Aioli, divided
(see Larder, page 138)
1 tablespoon Edamame Spread
(see Larder, page 139)
2 slices multigrain bread
5 ounces sliced roasted turkey
2 tablespoons onion sprouts
6 ¼-inch slices cucumber
5 slices jalapeño
2 tablespoons arugula
1 teaspoon cilantro
¼ of an avocado, sliced

Take one of the bread slices and slather with half of the Aioli and all of the Edamame Spread. Pile the turkey on top, then the onion sprouts, cucumber, jalapeño, arugula, cilantro, and finally the avocado. Spread the other slice of bread with remaining Aioli and place on top.

HAM & BUTTER SANDWICH

Preparation time: 5 minutes
Makes 1 serving

THE MOST SIMPLE SANDWICH IN MY COLLECTION HAS THE BIGGEST STORY. WAY BACK WHEN I WAS LIVING IN FRANCE, I HAD THE HONOR OF WORKING FOR GÉRARD MULOT AT HIS BEAUTIFUL BAKERY IN THE 6TH ARRONDISSEMENT. WE ARRIVED AT WORK IN THE MORNING WHEN IT WAS DARK AND LEFT AT NIGHT WHEN IT WAS DARK. I WAS A 5'10" WOMAN (THE ONLY WOMAN AT THE TIME) IN THE WINDOWLESS CAVE (BASEMENT), WHERE THE COUNTERS WENT UP TO MY MID-THIGH. DOWN THERE WERE A LOT OF PETITE FRENCH BAKERS AND TALL ME, WHO HAD A VERY POOR COMMAND OF THE LANGUAGE. AROUND NOON EVERY DAY, A LITTLE OLD WOMAN WITH A BASKET ON HER ARM WOULD WALK THROUGH THE KITCHEN AND THROW A SANDWICH ONTO MY PLAQUE. THIS WAS THE MOST INCREDIBLE THING I HAD EVER EATEN, AND YET SO SIMPLE: FRENCH HAM AND FRAGRANT, CREAMY BUTTER ON A FRESH BAGUETTE. THE MEMORIES OF THOSE TIMES IN MULOT'S KITCHEN ARE SEARED IN MY BRAIN AND ALWAYS COME BACK WHEN I EAT THIS SANDWICH. I'VE MADE IT FOR MY CHILDREN THEIR WHOLE LIVES, AND NOW ALL THE CHILDREN IN THE NEIGHBORHOOD LOVE IT, TOO. IT MAKES ME SO HAPPY TO SHARE THIS SIMPLE GOODNESS.

⅓ baguette, halved lengthwise
1 tablespoon premium butter, at room
   temperature
3 slices French ham (available at gourmet
   markets, Whole Foods, and online)

Slather the baguette with butter. Arrange ham slices between the baguette halves.

TEMPEH SANDWICH

Preparation time: 15 minutes, plus Aioli and Olive Tapenade
Cooking time: 5 minutes
Makes 1 serving

MY PRODUCE VENDOR INTRODUCED ME TO TEMPEH FIFTEEN YEARS AGO,
AND IT'S BEEN A PART OF MY FAMILY MEALS EVER SINCE. IT TURNS GOLDEN
BROWN AND NUTTY WHEN YOU SAUTE IT.

3 tablespoons olive oil
3 ¼-inch slices of tempeh
1 tablespoon Aioli (see Larder, page 138)
1 tablespoon Olive Tapenade
    (see Larder, page 140)
2 slices wheat bread
1 tablespoon onion sprouts
3 slices of pickle, cut lengthwise
2 slices tomato
1 tablespoon red onion, sliced paper thin
¼ of an avocado, thinly sliced
Salt to taste

Heat olive oil in a small skillet over medium high heat. Fry the
tempeh for a couple of minutes on each side until golden. Slather
one slice of bread with half of the Aioli and all of the tapenade.
Place the fried tempeh in a single layer on top of the tapenade.
Season with a pinch of salt. Place onion sprouts on top of the
tempeh, then the pickle, tomato, red onion, and finally the avocado.
Spread remaining Aioli on the other slice of bread and place on top.

Soups & Stews

Soup is good food, plain and simple. On cold school days, my kids love chicken noodle soup... for breakfast. The mix of warm broth, protein, and a few vegetables gets them straight through the morning. My family will eat soup at any meal, and so will our friends at Little Flower, so we make a lot of soups. Here are some favorites.

●━━━━━━━━━━━━━━━━━━━━━━━━━━━━●

CURRY VEGETABLE STEW

Preparation time: 40 minutes
Cooking time: 20 minutes
Makes 8-10 servings

THIS IS A GREAT RECIPE FOR CLEANING OUT THE VEGETABLE DRAWER. YOU SIMPLY THROW IT ALL TOGETHER AND ADD SOME YOGURT AND CURRY POWDER. USE THE CHUTNEY AS A GARNISH, OR IF YOU'RE LUCKY ENOUGH TO LIVE NEAR AN INDIAN MARKET, USE SALTY LIMES—THEY'RE DELICIOUS!

2 tablespoons olive oil
2 onions, chopped
2 shallots, finely chopped
1 bunch green onions, chopped, with white and green parts separated
5 carrots, peeled and cut into ½-inch slices
3 stalks celery, cut into ½-inch pieces
3 cloves garlic, peeled and minced
2 russet potatoes, peeled and cut into 1-inch pieces
3 zucchini, sliced into ½-inch thick rounds
¼ cup yellow curry powder
1 tablespoon turmeric
Water
2 cups kale leaves, torn
1 cup frozen peas
2 cups firmly packed fresh spinach leaves
3 cups plain whole-milk yogurt*
Salt and freshly ground pepper to taste

In a large pot, heat the olive oil and sauté the onions, shallots, white parts of the green onion, carrots, and celery until the onions are translucent and start to color, about 10 minutes. Stir in the garlic, potatoes, zucchini, curry powder, and turmeric and cook until the garlic is fragrant, about 2 minutes. Add just enough water to almost cover; the top layer of vegetables should be poking through the water's surface. Bring to a simmer and add kale. Continue to cook at a simmer until the carrots are fork tender, stirring occasionally. Remove from heat. Add the peas and spinach and stir until the spinach wilts. Stir in the yogurt. Season to taste with salt and pepper. Serve with brown rice and garnish with the reserved green parts of the green onion.

*Use whole-milk yogurt to ensure that the yogurt doesn't curdle in the hot liquid.

GREEN SOUP

Preparation time: 20 minutes
Cooking time: 20 minutes
Makes 6-8 servings

AS MY KIDS KNOW, I LIKE TO SAY "GOOD FOR YOU TODAY AND GOOD FOR YOU TOMORROW." THIS SOUP IS FRESH, GREEN, AND DELICIOUS.

1 bunch kale
1 tablespoons olive oil
2 onions, chopped
5 cloves garlic, peeled and minced
1 bunch asparagus, trimmed and cut into
   1-inch lengths
1 quart vegetable stock
3 cups water
1½ cups fresh spinach leaves
1 cup arugula
1 package (1 pound) frozen peas
Salt and freshly ground white pepper to
   taste

Remove and discard the tough center stalks of the kale. Tear the leaves by hand into large pieces and wash in cold water.

In a large pot, heat the olive oil and sauté the onion and garlic over medium heat until softened. Add the kale, asparagus, stock, and water and bring to a boil over medium-high heat. Turn the heat down to a simmer and cook until vegetables are tender, about 5 minutes. Remove from heat and add the spinach, arugula, and frozen peas. Blend to a smooth purée with an immersion blender or food processor. Add salt and white pepper to taste.

LEMON LENTIL SOUP

Preparation time: 10 minutes
Cooking time: 25 minutes
Makes 6-8 servings

THIS IS THE MOST POPULAR SOUP AT THE CAFÉ—CLEARLY I'M NOT THE ONLY
ONE WHO LOVES ANYTHING WITH LENTILS. THE LEMON JUICE MAKES IT
FRESH AND BRIGHT.

2½ quarts vegetable stock
4 cups lentils, picked over, rinsed, and
   drained
½ cup onion, finely chopped
¼ cup celery, finely chopped
¼ cup carrot, finely chopped
1 teaspoon turmeric
1 teaspoon minced garlic
2 teaspoons curry powder
½ teaspoon ground ginger
1 cup lemon juice
½ of one preserved lemon, finely chopped
Salt and freshly ground pepper to taste

Combine stock, lentils, onion, celery, carrot, turmeric, garlic, curry, and ginger in a large pot. Bring to a boil, then lower the heat to a simmer and cook, uncovered, until lentils are cooked through but still intact, about 20 minutes. Stir in the lemon juice, preserved lemon, and salt and pepper to taste, and serve.

Roasted Carrot & Fennel Soup

Preparation time: 30 minutes
Cooking time: 1 hour 15 minutes
Makes 6-8 servings

I ALWAYS HAVE CARROTS IN MY FRIDGE, PARTLY SO I CAN MAKE THIS SOUP
ON SHORT NOTICE. IF I DON'T HAVE FENNEL ON HAND, I USE ONIONS
INSTEAD—THAT'S ALSO DELICIOUS. YELLOW CARROTS WHEN IN SEASON MAKE
IT BEAUTIFUL, TOO.

1½ **pounds carrots, trimmed and peeled**
2 **tablespoons olive oil**
3 **fennel bulbs**
2 **tablespoons olive oil**
1 **tablespoon olive oil**
1 **onion, chopped**
2 **cloves garlic, peeled and minced**
1 **quart vegetable stock**
3 **cups water**
**Salt and freshly ground white pepper to
    taste**

Preheat the oven to 375°. Cut the carrots into 1-inch segments,
toss with 2 tablespoons olive oil, and spread in a single layer on a
baking sheet. Roast in the oven for until tender and nicely browned,
about 1 hour.

Meanwhile, trim off the fennel fronds and roots. Cut the bulbs into
¼-inch slices, submerge in cold water, drain, and pat dry. Toss with
2 tablespoons olive oil and spread out in single layer on a separate
baking sheet. Roast fennel in the same oven until tender and nicely
browned, about 30 minutes.

When the carrots and fennel are roasted, heat 1 tablespoon olive
oil in a large pot over medium-high heat. Add onion and sauté until
softened, about 4 minutes. Add garlic and cook for 30 seconds.
Add the roasted veggies, stock, and water. Bring to a boil over
medium-high heat. Blend to a smooth purée with an immersion
blender or food processor. Add salt and white pepper to taste.

ROASTED CAULIFLOWER & LEEK SOUP

Preparation time: 30 minutes
Cooking time: 1 hour
Makes 6-8 servings

THIS SOUP IS EASY, CREAMY, AND GOOD FOR YOU. PLUS IT TASTES GREAT. IF YOU DON'T HAVE LEEKS, NO PROBLEM—JUST USE ONIONS.

———————————————————————————————————————

**1 head cauliflower
2 tablespoons olive oil
3 leeks
1 tablespoon olive oil
1 quart vegetable stock
3 cups water
Salt and freshly ground white pepper to
    taste**

Preheat the oven to 375°. Break up the cauliflower into bite-size florets, rinse with water, pat dry, and toss with 2 tablespoons olive oil. Spread in a single layer on a baking sheet and bake until tender and nicely browned, about 45 minutes.

Meanwhile, remove the tough, dark green tops and roots of the leeks. Cut each leek in half lengthwise, then into ½ inch slices. Submerge completely in cold water to remove the grit, then drain and pat dry. Toss with 1 tablespoon olive oil and spread in single layer on a separate baking sheet. Roast in the same oven until tender and nicely browned, about 25 minutes.

Add roasted veggies, stock, and water to a large stock pot. Bring to a boil over medium-high heat. Blend to smooth purée with an immersion blender or food processor. Add salt and white pepper to taste.

SPANISH CHICKPEA SOUP

Preparation time: 15 minutes, plus Larder ingredients
Cooking time: 30 minutes
Makes 8-10 servings

HARRIET HAYES, A FRIEND, COOK, AND RECIPE TESTER EXTRAORDINAIRE, MADE THIS DELICIOUS SOUP FOR ME ONE DAY. I LOVED IT SO MUCH THAT WE MADE IT AT THE CAFÉ, AND IT QUICKLY BECAME A FAVORITE. THE SAUSAGE IS SO SATISFYING AND ADDS TONS OF FLAVOR. THANKS, HARRIET.

●————————————————————————————————●

¾ pound Italian sausage, removed
   from casings
1 tablespoon olive oil
½ cup roughly chopped onion
6 cloves garlic, roughly chopped
2 Roasted Red Peppers (see Larder,
   page 140), coarsely chopped
1½ cups Tomato Confit
   (see Larder, page 141)
1 quart chicken stock
1 cup water
2 tablespoons paprika
½ teaspoon coriander
¼ teaspoon cumin
¼ teaspoon cayenne pepper
1 large russet potato, peeled and
   cut into ½-inch cubes
1 bunch kale or spinach, rinsed,
   trimmed, and coarsely chopped
2 15-ounce cans garbanzo beans
   (chickpeas), rinsed and drained
Salt to taste

Brown sausage in 1 tablespoon of oil over medium-high heat. Using a slotted spoon, transfer sausage to a plate lined with paper towels to soak up excess grease. In the same pot, sauté onion in the residual oil over medium-high heat until softened, about 5 minutes. Add garlic and cook for another 30 seconds. Add the Roasted Red Pepper, Tomato Confit, stock, water, and spices to the pot. Bring to a boil, then lower to a simmer. Use an immersion blender to purée the soup in the pot until smooth. Add the potato, greens, and garbanzo beans to the simmering pot and cook until potatoes are tender, about 5 minutes. Season with salt to taste.

WHITE BEAN & KALE SOUP

Preparation time: 15 minutes
Cooking time: 20 minutes
Makes 6 servings

I LOVE KALE. UNFORTUNATELY, MY KIDS DON'T—AT LEAST NOT YET. LITTLE DO THEY KNOW THAT I SNEAK A GOOD DOSE INTO THIS CREAMY SOUP, WHICH HAPPENS TO BE VEGAN.

●———————————————————————————————————————●

1 bunch kale, any variety
2 tablespoons olive oil
2 cloves garlic, minced
2 tablespoons fresh thyme leaves
2 15-ounce cans white beans, rinsed and drained
1 quart vegetable stock
Salt and freshly ground white pepper

Remove and discard the tough center stalks of the kale. Tear the leaves by hand into large pieces and rinse in cold water.

In a large pot, heat the olive oil and sauté the kale over medium-high heat until wilted, about 3 minutes. Add the garlic and thyme and cook for another 2 minutes. Add the beans and stock and bring to a boil. Lower heat to a simmer and cook until the kale is very tender, about 15 minutes. Remove from heat and use the back of a spoon or a potato masher to break down some of the beans, making sure to leave some beans intact as well. Add salt and white pepper to taste.

SWEETS

Aaahh, you've found my weakness. After 30 years of baking, I've realized that I actually do have some favorites. Here are a few.

BLOOD ORANGE TART

Preparation time: 30 minutes, plus 20 minutes chilling time
and Quick Puff Pastry
Cooking time: 45 minutes
Makes two 9-inch tarts, 10 servings each

THIS TART WAS ON THE VERY FIRST PASTRY MENU AT THE CAFÉ. WE OPENED IN DECEMBER, AND THE BLOOD ORANGES THAT JANUARY WERE AMAZING—DARK AND POWERFULLY FLAVORFUL. CUSTOMERS ASK FOR THIS YEAR-ROUND.

●━━━●

1 recipe Quick Puff Pastry,
  thawed if frozen (see page 14)
½ cup butter, softened
1 cup plus 1 tablespoon sugar,
  divided
1 pinch salt
2 large eggs

1¼ cups finely ground almonds
1 tablespoon plus 1 teaspoon
  all-purpose flour
8 blood oranges
2 tablespoons cold butter, diced
1 egg, beaten

First, make a frangipane. Beat together the softened butter, ½ cup sugar, and salt until pale. Add the eggs one at a time, mixing between each addition. Mix in the almonds and flour until just combined. Set aside at room temperature.

To segment the oranges, use a sharp paring knife to slice off both ends of the fruit. Then remove both peel and pith by slicing downward and carefully following the curve of the fruit. Release the segments by cutting along either side of the connective membranes. Set aside the segments and all the juice.

On a lightly floured surface, roll out and trim each puff pastry sheet into a 15-inch round no more than ⅛ inch thick. Gently place each pastry circle onto a baking sheet lined with parchment paper or silicone that's been lightly greased. For each tart, take 1 cup frangipane and spread into a thin, even layer, leaving a 3-inch outer edge. Mound the orange segments over the frangipane, reserving the juice. Take the edge and fold inward to partially cover the center of the tart all the way around in 5 or 6 pleats. Freeze formed tarts until thoroughly chilled, at least 20 minutes.

Preheat oven to 350°. Dot the chilled tarts with the diced butter, brush the folded edge with the beaten egg, and sprinkle generously with ½ cup of sugar. Bake until pastry is a deep golden brown on top and bottom, about 45 minutes. In the meantime, heat the reserved orange juice and 1 tablespoon of sugar in a small saucepan over high heat until syrupy. Drizzle finished tarts with blood orange reduction before serving.

BROWN BUTTER CAKE
WITH APRICOT

Preparation time: 20 minutes, plus Perfect White Cakes and Brown Butter
Makes one 4-layer cake

ALL OF MY FAVORITE FLAVORS ARE WRAPPED UP IN ONE LOVELY PACKAGE IN
THIS CAKE.

●━━━●

**2 9-inch Perfect White Cakes
(see page 131)**

For the Cake Syrup:
⅓ **cup sugar**
⅔ **cup water**
1 tablespoon lemon juice

For the Brown Butter Buttercream:
**1 cup Brown Butter, room
temperature (see Larder,
page 139)**

**4 cups confectioner's sugar
3 tablespoons milk
¼ teaspoon salt**

For the Filling:
**1 cup apricot preserves,
room temperature
1 teaspoon lemon juice**

To make the cake syrup, combine sugar and water in a small saucepan and bring to a boil over high heat. Remove from heat and add lemon juice. Allow to cool to room temperature before using.

To make the buttercream frosting, beat together Brown Butter, sugar, milk, and salt at low speed with an electric mixer until sugar is fully incorporated. Scrape down sides of the bowl. Increase speed to high and mix until pale and fluffy.

To make the filling, thoroughly whisk together the apricot preserves and lemon juice.

Remove the completely cooled Perfect White Cakes from their pans by running a thin knife along the edge to loosen the sides and inverting the pan. Remove parchment. For each cake, use a serrated blade to trim off the domed top. Then cut into 2 even layers for a total of 4 layers.

Place the bottom cake layer on a cake plate. Moisten with ¼ cup of the cake syrup. Spread a thin layer of apricot preserves, about ⅓ cup. Gently place the next cake layer on top. Repeat 2 times. Top with 4th cake layer and moisten with remaining syrup. Use an offset spatula to spread the Brown Butter Buttercream over the top and sides of the cake.

BROWN BUTTER SHORTBREAD

Preparation time: 25 minutes, plus 1 hour chilling time
Cooking time: 20 minutes
Makes 18 servings

I DREAMT ABOUT THIS COOKIE FOR A MONTH. SHORTBREAD IS MY ABSOLUTE
FAVORITE. GROWING UP, I ALWAYS PICKED PECAN SANDIES AT THE A & P
WHEN IT WAS MY TURN. THIS SHORTBREAD IS NOW MY NEW FAVORITE. MAKE
SURE TO GET YOUR BUTTER NICE AND BROWN, AND SCRAPE THOSE BROWN
CRUMBLY BITS INTO THE BUTTER. THAT'S WHERE ALL THE FLAVOR IS!

---

1 cup Brown Butter, room temperature
(see Larder, page 139)
½ cup firmly packed light brown sugar
2 tablespoons granulated sugar
1 teaspoon vanilla extract
1 teaspoon salt
1¼ cups all-purpose flour
½ cup white rice flour
¼ cup turbinado sugar for sprinkling

In a stand mixer or with a hand mixer, mix together Brown Butter,
both sugars, vanilla, and salt. Add both types of flour to form a soft
dough. Remove from bowl and pat down into a ½-inch-thick flat
disk and wrap tightly in plastic. Chill thoroughly in the refrigerator
for at least 1 hour.

Preheat the oven to 350°. Generously grease the tins of two
cupcake pans with butter or cooking spray. On a lightly floured
surface, cut the chilled dough into 2-inch circles with the rim of a
glass or biscuit cutter. Place each circle in cupcake tin and bake
until edges are golden, about 15 minutes. Sprinkle each shortbread
with a generous pinch of the turbinado sugar. Bake for another 5
minutes. Set aside for 15 minutes to cool slightly. Then run a small
thin knife all the way around the sides of each tin to remove each
cookie. It's easier to remove the cookies from the pan when they're
still warm but are cool enough to handle.

BROWNIE CUPS

Preparation time: 25 minutes
Cooking time: 15 minutes
Makes 24 servings

NOT TOO SWEET AND A BIT FUDGY. MY FAVORITE BROWNIE EVER.

●━━━━━━━━━━━━━━━━━━━━━━━━━━━━━━━━━━━●

1 cup chopped unsweetened chocolate
1 cup semi-sweet chocolate chips
1 cup butter
5 large eggs
1 cup granulated sugar
1½ cups firmly packed light brown sugar
2 teaspoons vanilla extract
1¼ cup all-purpose flour
1½ teaspoons baking powder
1 teaspoon salt

Preheat oven to 325°. Line two cupcake tins with paper cups. Place both types of chocolate and butter in a heatproof bowl set over a pot of simmering water. Heat gently, stirring occasionally, until completely melted and smooth, then remove from heat. Set aside and allow to cool slightly for 5 minutes.

In a separate large bowl, whisk the eggs, sugars, and vanilla. Fold the chocolate into the egg mixture. In a separate small bowl, combine the flour, baking powder, and salt. Then fold the flour mixture into the chocolate-egg mixture. Fill the prepared tins ¾ full and bake for about 15 minutes, rotating pans halfway through for even cooking. They're ready when the edges puff and the surface starts to crack. A toothpick inserted in the middle should come out with a moist, fudgy crumb sticking to it.

CHOCOLATE CHIP COOKIES

Preparation time: 15 minutes, plus 1 hour chilling time
Cooking time: 12-15 minutes
Makes 3½ dozen

THIS RECIPE CAME FROM DAVID WYNNS. I WORKED FOR DAVID AT LES DEUX CAFÉS IN HOLLYWOOD. HE WOULD ALWAYS COME INTO THE KITCHEN WHEN THESE COOKIES WERE WARM OUT OF THE OVEN AND STAND NEXT TO THE COOLING RACK AND DEVOUR AT LEAST HALF A DOZEN. ONE TIME HE CALLED ME FROM PARIS IN THE MIDDLE OF THE NIGHT BECAUSE HE NEEDED THE RECIPE ASAP. DAVID CHANGED MY LIFE.

●━━●

1 cup butter, room temperature
1 cup firmly packed light brown sugar
1 cup granulated sugar
2 large eggs
1½ teaspoons vanilla extract
2½ cups all-purpose flour
1½ teaspoons baking soda
1 teaspoon salt
2 cups semi-sweet chocolate chips, mini
    or regular size

Beat the butter and both sugars together until creamy and pale. Mix in the eggs one by one and then the vanilla. Scrape down the sides of the bowl. In a separate bowl, combine the flour, baking soda, and salt. Mix the flour mixture into the butter-sugar mixture until barely combined. Add the chocolate chips and mix until evenly distributed. Form into 1½-inch balls and slightly flatten each with your palm. Place on a baking sheet lined with parchment paper or a silicone mat, side by side. Chill thoroughly in the freezer, for at least 1 hour. May store in the freezer for up to a week.

When you're ready to bake, preheat the oven to 350°. Space the frozen cookies on new lined baking sheets 2 inches apart, 12 per sheet. Bake until the edges just start to turn golden and the middle is still pale, 12 to 15 minutes.

CHOCOLATE BLACK SESAME BOUCHONS

Preparation time: 25 minutes
Cooking time: 20-25 minutes
Makes 18 bouchons or 12 individual cakes

CHOCOLATE AND SESAME IS A WONDERFUL FLAVOR COMBINATION. THESE BOUCHONS ARE CHEWY AND DELICIOUS.

⅓ **cup black sesame seeds**
¾ **cup butter**
¼ **cup sesame oil**
½ **cup granulated sugar**
1 **cup firmly packed light brown sugar**
1½ **cups Dutch process cocoa powder**
1 **tablespoon instant espresso powder**
½ **teaspoon salt**
3 **eggs**
¾ **cup all-purpose flour**
¼ **teaspoon white sesame seeds & ¼ teaspoon black sesame seeds, combined**

Toast ⅓ cup black sesame seeds on the stove over medium-low heat, stirring continuously. Remove from heat when seeds start to pop. Grind sesame seeds in a mortar and pestle or food processor into a coarse powder.

Preheat oven to 325°. Using a pastry brush or your fingers, generously grease the tins of a cupcake pan or 18 bouchon tins (of a typical 24) in two silicone bouchon molds with soft butter. Place butter, sesame oil, both sugars, cocoa powder, espresso powder, and salt in a saucepan and cook over low heat until the butter melts. Remove from heat and scrape the batter into a large mixing bowl. Whisk in the eggs one at a time until incorporated. Mix in flour and ground sesame until just combined. Scoop into prepared tins. Sprinkle the black and white sesame seed mixture on top of each cake. Bake about 25 minutes for the cupcakes or 20 minutes for the bouchons. They're done when a toothpick inserted in the middle comes out with a moist crumb sticking to it. Cool completely before removing from pan.

COCONUT MACAROONS

Preparation time: 10 minutes, plus 1 hour chilling time
Cooking time: 15-20 minutes
Makes 3 dozen

THESE ARE FLAKY, CHEWY, MELT-IN-YOUR-MOUTH COOKIES. YOU CAN ADD
SOME CANDIED GINGER IF YOU'RE FEELING ADVENTUROUS.

———

3 egg whites
1⅓ cups sugar
1 teaspoon vanilla extract
4 cups shredded sweetened coconut
¾ cup all-purpose flour

Combine the egg whites and sugar in a heatproof bowl and place
over a pot of simmering water. Cook, stirring occasionally, until
the egg white-sugar mixture is warm like bath water and the sugar
has dissolved. Stir in the vanilla, coconut, and flour. When it binds
together, remove from the heat. Form dough into 1¼-inch balls.
Place side by side on a baking sheet lined with parchment paper or
a silicone mat. Wrap tightly with plastic wrap and chill in the freezer
for at least 1 hour. May keep in the freezer for up to a week.

When you're ready to bake the cookies, preheat oven to 350°.
Space the frozen cookies on lined baking sheets 1 inch apart. Bake
until the macaroons turn golden, 15 to 20 minutes.

FOLEY CAKE

Preparation time: 20 minutes
Cooking time: 70 minutes
Makes one 8-inch cake, 8-10 servings

I USED TO BELONG TO A CHEESE CLUB—BASICALLY, IT WAS A BUNCH OF FUN FRIENDS WHO USED EATING CHEESE AS AN EXCUSE TO GET TOGETHER. ONE NIGHT, STEPHANIE FOLEY MADE THIS DELICIOUS CAKE, AND WHEN I GOT HOME I THOUGHT ABOUT IT ALL NIGHT. SHE GRACIOUSLY LET ME PUT IT ON THE MENU AT THE CAFÉ. WE ADDED SOME NUTS AND JAM AND A FEW MORE THINGS BUT NAMED IT FOLEY CAKE AFTER HER. THANKS, STEPH.

1 cup butter, melted and cooled
2 cups sugar
3 large eggs
2 teaspoons vanilla extract
2 teaspoons almond extract
2 cups all-purpose flour
1 teaspoons salt
½ cup raspberry or apricot jam
½ cup sliced almonds

Preheat the oven to 350°. Grease an 8-inch cake pan with butter or cooking spray and line with parchment paper that's been trimmed to fit the bottom of the pan. Using a stand mixer or hand blender and a large bowl, mix the melted butter and sugar together until combined. Add the eggs and both types of extracts and mix until smooth. Fold in the flour and salt. Pour half of the batter into the prepared pan and smooth out. Spread the fruit jam into an even layer atop the batter, leaving an outer half-inch margin. Pour the remaining cake batter over the top and smooth out. Top with sliced almonds. At this point, you can either wrap the cake tightly in plastic wrap and refrigerate for up to 1 week or bake immediately. Bake for the first 40 minutes at 350°. Reduce the oven temperature to 300° and continue to bake until a toothpick inserted in the middle comes out with a moist crumb sticking to it, about 30 more minutes.

GINGER MOLASSES COOKIES

Preparation time: 25 minutes, plus 1 hour chilling time
Cooking time: 10 minutes
Makes 2 dozen

THESE COOKIES COME OUT CHEWY AND PERFECT EVERY TIME. YOU CAN
FREEZE THE PORTIONED DOUGH BALLS AND BAKE THEM WHENEVER YOU
WANT. DON'T FORGET TO ROLL THEM IN SUGAR FIRST.

⸻

¾ cup Brown Butter, room temperature
   (see Larder, page 139)
¼ cup firmly packed light brown sugar
½ cup granulated sugar
1 large egg
¼ cup molasses
2 teaspoons grated fresh ginger
2 cups all-purpose flour
2 teaspoons baking soda
½ teaspoon salt
1 teaspoon ground ginger
1 teaspoon ground cinnamon
½ teaspoon ground cloves
1 tablespoon finely chopped candied
   ginger
½ cup granulated sugar for rolling

Using a stand mixer or hand blender, beat the brown butter and
both sugars together until creamy and pale. Mix in the egg,
molasses, and fresh ginger. Scrape down the sides of the bowl. In a
separate bowl, combine the flour, baking soda, salt, ground spices,
and candied ginger. Add the flour-spice mixture to the butter-sugar-
egg mixture and mix until just combined. Form dough into 1½-inch
balls and slightly flatten with your palm. Roll in granulated sugar
to coat evenly and place side by side on baking sheet lined with
parchment paper or a silicone mat. Chill thoroughly in the freezer
for at least 1 hour. May keep in the freezer for up to a week.

When you're ready to bake the cookies, preheat the oven to 350°.
Space the frozen cookies on lined baking sheets 2 inches apart,
12 per sheet. Bake until the surface of the cookies starts to crack
and the center is still very soft, about 10 minutes.

GLAZED NUTS

Preparation time: 15 minutes
Cooking time: 15-20 minutes
Makes 24 servings

A FUN AND EASY HOLIDAY TREAT, THESE NUTS MAKE A GREAT GIFT. ADD
SOME CURRY FOR AN EXTRA KICK!

---

1 egg white
2 teaspoons salt
¾ cup confectioner's sugar
½ teaspoon ground cayenne pepper
1 teaspoon ground cinnamon
2 tablespoons fresh rosemary leaves,
   coarsely chopped
2 cups raw pecans
2 cups raw cashews
2 cups raw almonds
2 cups raw walnuts

Preheat oven to 350°. Line 2 baking sheets with parchment paper
or a silicone mat. In a large bowl, stir together the egg white, salt,
confectioner's sugar, cayenne pepper, cinnamon, and rosemary.
Add the nuts and mix thoroughly. Divide the nuts evenly between
the 2 prepared pans, spreading into a single layer. Bake for 15 to
20 minutes, rotating the pans and stirring the nuts halfway through
for even cooking. Cool completely before storing in an airtight
container.

Variation: Curried Glazed Nuts

Use 1 tablespoon mild curry powder and ½ teaspoon ground ginger
in place of the cinnamon and rosemary. After baking and when the
nuts are completely cooled, stir in 1 cup of raisins.

LOLLIPOPS

Preparation time: 15 minutes
Cooking time: 10 minutes
Makes 24 servings

THESE LOLLIPOPS ARE EASY TO MAKE AND BEAUTIFUL! THEY'RE REALLY
FUN TO MAKE WITH THE KIDS AROUND THE HOLIDAYS. I USE ALL KINDS
OF HOLIDAY CANDIES AND COOKIE DECORATIONS. SILVER DRAGEES ARE
ALSO BEAUTIFUL. YOU CAN CUSTOMIZE THEM FOR ANY OCCASION. JUST BE
CAREFUL AROUND THE KIDS—THE CANDY IS MOLTEN LAVA.

**Assorted hard candies, licorice, sanding
    sugar, and sprinkles
2 cups sugar
⅔ cup corn syrup
½ cup water
24 lollipop sticks**

Generously grease two mini cupcake tins with cooking spray. Fill
the bottom of each tin with half a teaspoon of various candies,
sanding sugar, or sprinkles. In a large saucepan, melt the sugar,
corn syrup, and water over medium-high heat without stirring.
Once the mixture starts to boil, turn the heat down to medium
and continue to cook without stirring to 300° (hard crack stage),
checking with a candy thermometer. Use a large soup spoon to fill
the prepared tins with the molten syrup. Keep a bowl of ice water
nearby in case the syrup comes in contact with your skin. Allow the
lollipops to partially cool and set before inserting the sticks in the
center of the pops. Remove from the tins once completely cool.

Mini Caramel Apples

Preparation time: 15 minutes
Cooking time: 5 minutes
Makes about 20 servings

SUPER CUTE AND FUN TO MAKE WHEN LITTLE APPLES ARE IN SEASON. LOOK
FOR SOME DECORATIVE STICKS, TOO.

●━━━━━━━━━━━━━━━━━━━━━━━━━━━━━━━━●

**2 cups (1 pound) Little Flower
Sea Salt Caramels or other
good-quality caramels
1 pound whole crab apples or
other small apples
20 small popsicle sticks**

Place parchment paper or a silicone mat on a baking sheet and
grease generously with butter or cooking spray. Insert a popsicle
stick into the middle of each apple through the stem side. Melt
the caramel over medium heat in a large saucepan until uniformly
smooth, stirring occasionally to ensure even cooking. Pour the
caramel into a small, deep, heatproof bowl. Keep a bowl of ice
water nearby in case your skin comes in contact with the molten
caramel. Dunk each apple into the caramel to coat and place on the
prepared baking sheet to cool.

PEAR & QUINCE CRUMBLE

Preparation time: 25 minutes
Cooking time: 30 minutes, plus 90 minutes poaching time
Makes 12-14 servings

QUINCE IS THE CROWN JEWEL OF FALL FRUITS. ITS PINK-AMBER COLOR
AFTER COOKING IS A TRUE GIFT TO ANY FIRST-TIME QUINCE BAKER.
COMBINED WITH PEAR, IT MAKES FOR THE PERFECT CRUMBLE.

For the Streusel:
1½ cups all-purpose flour
¾ cup sugar
¾ cup firmly packed light
   brown sugar
½ teaspoon salt
1 cup cold butter, cut into
   1-inch cubes

For the Poached Quince:
3 quince

1 vanilla bean, scraped
Water

For the Fruit Filling:
Poached quince
5 pears, peeled, cored, and
   cut into 1-inch pieces
1 pinch salt
1 tablespoon lemon juice
½ cup sugar, plus more if
   desired to taste

Io prepare the streusel, mix together flour, both sugars, and salt. Cut the butter cubes into the flour mixture by pinching them with your fingers or mixing with the paddle attachment of a stand mixer at low speed until the butter forms pea-size lumps. Set aside to chill in the refrigerator.

To poach the quince, peel, core, and cut each quince into 1-inch pieces. Place the quince, vanilla bean pod, and vanilla seeds in a large pot. Cover with 2 inches of water and bring to a boil. Lower heat to a simmer and cook until fork tender and a deep rosy hue, up to 90 minutes. Remove the quince with a slotted spoon, reserving the poaching liquid for another use. Combine the poached quince, pear, salt, lemon juice, and sugar to taste (start with ½ cup) in a mixing bowl.

Preheat oven to 350°. Generously grease a 9 x 13-inch baking dish with butter or cooking spray. Spread the fruit filling in an even layer on the bottom. Spread streusel evenly over the fruit, squeezing the topping in your hand to create larger crumbles. Bake until the crumble topping is golden and the fruit juices are bubbling, about 30 minutes.

Variation: White Peach Crumble

For the fruit filling, use 3 pounds of white peaches instead of the quince and pear. Wash and cut the fruit into 1-inch pieces, removing the pits. Combine fruit, 1 pinch salt, 1 tablespoon lemon juice, and sugar to taste (start with ½ cup).

PERFECT WHITE CAKE

Preparation time: 30 minutes
Cooking time: 35-40 minutes
Makes two 9-inch cakes

THE TITLE SAYS IT ALL.

---

6 large eggs, separated
2½ cups plus 2 teaspoons
**   sugar, divided**
1½ cups butter, room
**   temperature**
1 tablespoon vanilla extract
3¾ cups cake flour
2 teaspoons baking powder
¾ teaspoon salt
1½ cups milk

Preheat oven to 350°. Grease cake pans with butter or cooking spray and line with parchment paper that's been trimmed to fit the bottom of the pan. Using an electric mixer, whip the egg whites with 1½ cups of the sugar at high speed until the peaks are stiff and glossy. Set aside. In a separate large bowl, beat together the butter and remaining sugar until pale. Add the egg yolks and vanilla to the butter mixture, scraping down the sides of the bowl a couple times during mixing. In a third bowl, combine flour, baking powder, and salt. Add one third of the flour mixture into the butter-egg mixture and mix at low speed until combined. Then add half the milk. Scrape down the sides of the bowl. Repeat. Then mix in the last third of the flour mixture and gently fold in the whipped egg whites until just combined. Pour batter into prepared pans. Bake until a toothpick inserted in the middle of the cake comes out clean, about 30 minutes. Rotate pan halfway through bake time for even cooking. Allow the cakes to cool at least 30 minutes in the pan before turning them out, removing the parchment, and placing them right side up.

If not using immediately, wrap the cakes tightly with plastic wrap after they've completely cooled and freeze for up to 2 weeks.

For a simple presentation, prepare a glaze by whisking together 1 cup confectioner's sugar, 2 tablespoons lemon juice, and the zest of 1 lemon until smooth. Pour over the center of one cake layer and allow it to fall as it will over the top and sides. Sprinkle with 2 teaspoons of lavender.

131

PUMPKIN BREAD PUDDING WITH SALTY CARAMEL SAUCE

Preparation time: 25 minutes, plus 15 minutes soaking time
Cooking time: 50 minutes
Makes 10-12 servings

MY GREAT FRIEND DEB LIVES FOR THIS BREAD PUDDING. I CAN'T THINK
OF A BETTER USE FOR ALL THAT LEFTOVER BREAD—AND IT'S A LOVELY
ALTERNATIVE TO TRADITIONAL HOLIDAY PIES.

8 cups day-old crusty bread, cut into
   2-inch cubes
1 15-ounce can pumpkin
2½ cups heavy cream, divided
1 cup milk
1 cup sugar
4 large eggs
2 egg yolks
½ teaspoon salt
1 teaspoon cinnamon
½ teaspoon ginger
¼ teaspoon allspice
⅛ teaspoon cloves
¼ pound (about 1 cup) Little Flower
   Sea Salt Caramels or other good-
   quality caramels

Preheat oven to 350°. Arrange bread cubes in a single layer on a
baking sheet. Bake until bread starts to color, about 15 minutes.
Generously grease 9- x13-inch casserole with butter or cooking
spray. Arrange toasted bread cubes in a single layer in the
prepared casserole. Whisk together pumpkin, 2 cups cream, milk,
sugar, egg yolks, salt, and spices in a large mixing bowl. Strain the
custard through a sieve before pouring into prepared casserole. Let
soak for 15 minutes. Cover tightly with aluminum foil and bake for 25
minutes. Remove cover and return to oven to bake until custard is set,
about 25 more minutes.

When pudding is almost finished baking, melt the caramel with
½ cup cream in a small saucepan over medium-low heat. Stir
occasionally. Remove from heat when caramel has completely
melted. Pour over the pudding as soon as it comes out of the oven.

THUMBPRINT CHOCOLATE CARAMEL TARTLETS

Preparation time: 30 minutes, plus 20 minutes chilling time
Cooking time: 10-12 minutes
Makes 24 servings

THE RICE FLOUR GIVES THIS CHOCOLATE DOUGH A LITTLE SNAP. ADD THE
SALTY CARAMEL, AND YOU'VE GOT QUITE THE CHEWY TREAT.

For the Chocolate Crust
½ cup butter,
   room temperature
½ cup granulated sugar
1 egg
½ teaspoon vanilla extract
½ teaspoon salt
¾ cup all-purpose flour
¼ cup white rice flour
¼ cup plus 2 tablespoons
   cocoa powder

For the Caramel
¼ pound Little Flower Sea
   Salt Caramels, or other
   good-quality caramels
3 tablespoons cream

For the Ganache
½ cup heavy cream
1 cup coarsely chopped
   bittersweet chocolate
Sea salt for sprinkling

To prepare the crusts, use butter or cooking spray to generously grease the tins of 2 mini cupcake pans. In a large bowl, beat the butter and sugar together until pale yellow. Add the egg, vanilla, and salt and mix thoroughly In a separate small bowl, mix both types of flour and cocoa together and then stir them into the butter and egg mixture. Mix until the dough is smooth. Form the dough into ¾-inch balls and press firmly into the bottom of the tins with your thumb, leaving a deep well in the center. Chill the thumbprints in the freezer for 20 minutes. Preheat the oven to 350°. Bake until crust appears dry, 7 to 10 minutes. Remove from the oven and use the handle of a wooden spoon to press down the wells again. Set aside to completely cool, then remove from the pan.

For the caramel filling, melt the caramels and the cream in a saucepan over medium-low heat. Stir briefly after the caramels melt to fully incorporate the caramel and cream. Fill each thumbprint with ½ teaspoon of caramel.

For the ganache, bring the cream just to a boil over medium-low heat in a small saucepan. Remove from heat and pour over the chopped chocolate, allowing it to sit for a minute. Whisk the chocolate and cream together until smooth and shiny.

Top off each caramel-filled thumbprint with the chocolate and smooth out the surface with one swipe of an offset spatula. Set aside to cool at room temperature and sprinkle with a few grains of sea salt just before the chocolate is set.

THE LITTLE FLOWER LARDER

I'M A BUSY MOM WITH THREE KIDS. I CAN'T COOK EVERY NIGHT, BUT I CAN ASSEMBLE. SO I KEEP A WELL-STOCKED PANTRY AND COOK A FEW TIMES A WEEK, STOCKPILING COMPONENTS SO LATER ON I CAN EASILY THROW TOGETHER DINNER—OR EVEN A PARTY. THE ITEMS IN MY PANTRY LIST AND THE QUICK LARDER RECIPES WILL HELP YOU PUT TOGETHER MANY OF THE DISHES IN THE BOOK.

Pantry Items

For the Cupboard

Anchovies

Black sesame seeds

Dark sesame oil

Kalamata olives

Little Flower Sea Salt Caramels*

Maggi Seasoning Sauce

Preserved lemons

Rice flour

available at littleflowercandyco.com

For the Fridge

Butter, the good stuff

Curry powder

French ham

Fresh herbs

I keep on hand basil, chive, cilantro, dill, Italian flat-leaf

parsley, mint, rosemary, tarragon, and thyme; keep dried on hand in case you run out of fresh

Lavender

Nori

Spanish goat cheese

Kitchen Equipment

Baking sheets (2)

Bouchon molds (2)

Cake pan, 8-inch round

Cupcake tins (2)

Gratin dishes, 8-ounce capacity (2)

Japanese mandoline

Loaf pan, 9 inches x 5 inches

Lollipop sticks

Microplane grater

Mini muffin tins (2)

Offset spatula, small

Popsicle sticks, mini

Pots & pans: the basic set

LARDER BASICS

Aioli

In a large bowl, whisk together 4 egg yolks and 2 cloves minced garlic. Slowly stream 2¾ cups extra-virgin olive oil into the egg yolk mixture, whisking constantly. Mix in ⅓ cup lemon juice to thin out the aioli. Salt to taste. Makes about 3 cups.

Apricot Chutney

Chop 2 pounds of dried apricots into quarters, and dice half of a red bell pepper and half of a red onion into ¼-inch pieces. Combine the apricot, red bell, and onion with 1 cup sugar, 2 cups apple cider vinegar, and 3 cups water in a large pot. Bring to a boil, then lower the heat to simmer. Cook uncovered, stirring occasionally, until the apricots break down and the chutney thickens to a jam-like consistency. Remove from heat and add an additional ½ cup of apple cider vinegar at the end.

Baked Tofu

Drain, pat dry, and press two 14-ounce packages of extra-firm tofu between two plates weighed down by a heavy can. Set aside for 1 hour to remove excess moisture. Preheat oven to 350°. Mix 2 tablespoons dark sesame oil, ¾ cup soy sauce and ¾ cup water in a baking dish. Cut each tofu block into thirds (approximately 1-inch wide segments) and add to the marinade. Bake in a single layer for 40 minutes, turning over every 10 minutes. Store in the refrigerator for up to 1 week.

Barley

Wash and drain 1 cup barley once in cold water. Combine barley, 3 cups water, and ½ teaspoon salt in a large pot. Bring to a boil and lower heat to a gentle simmer. Cook covered until tender, about 40 minutes. Remove from heat and set aside, still covered, for another 10 minutes. Drain off any excess water.

Black-eyed Peas

Carefully pick over and rinse 2 cups of dried black-eyed peas. Cover with cold water and soak for at least 4 hours. Drain and place in a large pot. Cover with water by 2 inches. Bring to a boil and lower to a simmer until the peas are tender, about 30 minutes.

Blanched French Green Beans (Haricots Verts)

Cook trimmed French green beans in a pot of boiling water for 2 minutes until they're bright green. Promptly drain and plunge into ice water to stop the cooking.

Bread Crumbs

Preheat the oven to 350°. Tear day-old bread into 1-inch chunks, drizzle with olive oil, and bake until the bread is thoroughly dried out and golden. In a food processor, pulse the bread with some Parmesan cheese and parsley. Salt to taste. Once cooled, store in an airtight container.

Brown Butter

Melt 2 cups of butter in a large saucepan over medium heat. The melted butter will come to a foam. Start stirring frequently at this point until the butter foams a second time and the butter solids are a deep chocolate brown. Remove from heat. You should have about 1½ cups of brown butter on hand. Set aside to cool before using.

Brown Rice

Wash and drain 1½ cups short-grain brown rice at least three times in cold water. Combine rice, 2¼ cups water, and 1½ teaspoons salt in a large pot. Bring to a boil and then lower heat to a gentle simmer. Cook covered and undisturbed for 20 minutes. Remove from heat and set aside, still covered, for another 10 minutes. Fluff with fork before serving. Makes 4 servings.

Bulgur

Place 1 cup bulgur and ½ teaspoon salt in a heatproof bowl. Add enough boiling water to just cover the grains and set aside until tender, about 15 minutes. Drain any excess water if necessary. Season with more salt to taste.

Edamame Spread

Add one 10-ounce package of frozen shelled edamame to a pot of boiling water and cook until softened, about 3 minutes. Drain and set aside to cool to room temperature. Pulse the edamame with 2 tablespoons coarsely chopped garlic and 1½ cups extra-virgin olive oil. Season to taste with salt and pepper.

Hard-boiled Eggs

Gently place eggs in a single layer on the bottom of a saucepan and cover with cold water by 2 inches. Bring to a boil, remove from heat, and let stand, covered, for 10 minutes. Transfer the eggs to a bowl of ice water to stop the cooking.

Herbed Bread Crumbs

Preheat the oven to 350°. Line a baking sheet with parchment paper or a silicone mat. Cut 4 1-inch-thick slices of stale bread into 1-inch cubes. Toss with 2 tablespoons olive oil, 1 pinch salt, and 1 tablespoon finely chopped fresh parsley. Spread into a single layer on the baking sheet and bake until golden brown, about 15 minutes. Stir halfway through the cooking time to ensure even cooking. After the bread cubes have cooled, pulse in a food processor to a very coarse grind. Alternatively, break up the bread by placing it in a sealable plastic bag and crushing with a rolling pin. Mix the crumbs with 1 tablespoon grated Parmesan cheese.

Melted Leeks

Remove the tough, dark green tops and roots of 4 to 5 leek stalks. Halve the leeks lengthwise and cut into

½-inch slices. Wash thoroughly in a large bowl of cold water, allowing the sand to settle to the bottom of the bowl. Heat 1 tablespoon olive oil in a large skillet over medium heat and add the leeks. Stir frequently and cook gently until the leeks soften and turn golden, about 20 minutes. Add a couple of tablespoons of water to deglaze the pan.

Olive Tapenade
Pulse 2 cups pitted Kalamata olives, 3 peeled garlic cloves, and 1 tablespoon capers in a food processor until smooth.

Red Quinoa
Wash and drain 1 cup red quinoa at least three times in cold water. Combine quinoa, 1½ cups water, and ½ teaspoon salt in a medium pot. Bring to a boil, then lower heat to a gentle simmer. Cook covered and undisturbed for 20 minutes. Remove from heat and set aside, still covered, for another 10 minutes. Fluff with fork before serving.

Roasted Asparagus
Preheat oven to 400°. Rinse 1 bunch of asparagus and trim off the tough ends. Toss spears in 2 tablespoons olive oil and 1 generous pinch of salt. Arrange in a single layer on a baking sheet and bake until tender-crisp, about 15 minutes.

Roasted Red Pepper
Preheat oven to 400°. Wash 2 to 4 red bell peppers and pat dry. Toss in a light coat of olive oil, about 1 tablespoon. Arrange in a single layer on a baking dish and bake until the skin chars, 20 to 30 minutes. Rotate the bell peppers a couple of times while they cook to ensure even charring. Remove from oven and immediately transfer to a heatproof bowl. Cover tightly with plastic wrap and set aside until peppers are cool enough to handle. Discard skin, stems and seeds. The skin should slide right off.

Roasted Broccolini
Preheat oven to 400°. Rinse 2 bunches of broccolini and trim off the tough ends of the stems. Blanch in a pot of boiling water for 2 minutes until a vibrant green. Drain and toss in 2 tablespoons olive oil. Arrange in a single layer on a baking sheet and bake until the tips start to brown and the stems are tender-crisp, about 10 minutes.

Sautéed Mushrooms
Wipe off any grit from 1 pound of mushrooms with a clean, dry towel. Cut into ¼-inch slices. Heat 2 tablespoons olive oil in a large skillet over medium-high heat. Spread the mushrooms in a single layer in the hot pan, cooking in batches if necessary. Allow the mushrooms to brown thoroughly on one side without stirring. Then stir briefly to brown the mushrooms on the other side. Add 3 cloves minced garlic and cook for 1 minute. Season to taste with salt.

Sautéed Spinach

Thoroughly wash, rinse and drain 2 bunches of fresh spinach (6 to 8 cups of firmly packed leaves). Heat 2 tablespoons olive oil over medium-high heat in a large pan. Add the spinach to the pan (in batches if necessary) and stir quickly until the leaves just start to wilt. Add 3 cloves minced garlic to the pan and cook for a few more seconds until fragrant. Remove from heat and salt to taste.

Tomato Confit

Preheat oven to 350°. Wash and drain 2 pints of yellow and/or red cherry tomatoes. Combine the tomatoes with 4 peeled garlic cloves, fresh thyme leaves from 3 sprigs, 2 tablespoons olive oil, and 1½ teaspoons salt. Bake until most of the juice has evaporated and the tomatoes have collapsed and browned. Stir occasionally to ensure even cooking.

Wheat Berries

Wash and drain 1 cup wheat berries once in cold water. Combine wheat berries, 3 cups water, and 1 teaspoon salt in a medium pot. Bring to a boil, then lower heat to a gentle simmer. Cook, covered, until the wheat berries are firm-tender (al dente), about 1 hour. Remove from heat and drain well.

Abundant Thanks

To: Colleen Dunn Bates, my editor and publisher. Patience, freedom, and understanding is what you gave to me and this project. Thank you for the opportunity.

To: Rachel Vourlas Schacht, my book designer and friend. Thank you for going down this road with me—you're amazing.

To: Ryan Miller, my photographer. Your photos are art. Thank you for holding my hand.

To: Harriet Hayes, who tested all the recipes and made them all work. Thank you for your collaboration, for keeping me sane, and for being there every step of the way.

To: Eric Pfleeger, for your cover design and friendship, and for looking so good in navy.

To: Nancy Roberts Ransohoff, for your cookbook expertise and meticulous proofreading.

To: Cecilia Leung and Stephanie Luii, for being the most dedicated bakers ever, and for all the extra hours.

To: Roy Morris and Amanda Millett, for being real people and keeping it real.

To: Friedrich Kunath, for your wonderful sketch and your friendship.

To: Sara Fairchild-Nance, for your supportive friendship and for reading recipes.

To: Sumi Chang, for the phone call that brought the keys to happiness, and for your incredibe bread.

To: Dan Mys. No one will ever take your place on the line.

To: My devoted staff at Little Flower, for being humble servants. I am forever grateful.

To: Lennie LaGuire, for the feng shui, hard work, and the maple oat scone.

To: Ashley Johnson and Holly Jones. The two best girls ever!

To: Karen Hillenburg, Mike and Stephanie Bollenbacher, Alison Bogle, Mary McConnell, Andrea Shaffer, and Marguerite Rangle, for getting us off the ground, making us look good, and always coming to see me.

To: Chris Pollan, for always checking in.

To: Pamela Perkins, for walking in and never leaving.

To: Erin Linsin, for all the late nights.

To: Craig Cooper, for believing in me.

To: Barbara Sheridan, my mother, for teaching me to stand strong in the storm, and for letting me be next to you at the red table.

To: All the wonderful people who walk through the doors of this little café every day. We are all grateful.

INDEX